At Ganapati's Feet

Daily Life with the Elephant-Headed Deity

At Ganapati's Feet

Daily Life with the Elephant-Headed Deity

Janyananda Saraswati
(David Dillard-Wright)

MANTRA BOOKS

Winchester, UK
Washington, USA

First published by Mantra Books, 2014
Mantra Books is an imprint of John Hunt Publishing Ltd., Laurel House, Station Approach,
Alresford, Hants, SO24 9JH, UK
office1@jhpbooks.net
www.johnhuntpublishing.com
www.mantra-books.net

For distributor details and how to order please visit the 'Ordering' section on our website.

ISBN: 978 1 78099 099 6

A CIP catalogue record for this book is available from the British Library.

Design: Lee Nash

Printed and bound by CPI Group (UK) Ltd, Croydon, CR0 4YY

CONTENTS

Salutations to Lord Vinayaka, the remover of obstacles, whose gracious presence removes all fear.
Salutations to Saraswati, Durga, Kali, and Lakshmi, faces of the Divine Mother, who destroy egotism and inspire speech.
Salutations to Ramakrishna and Sarada Ma, Shree Maa of Kamakhya, and Swami Satyananda Saraswati, the lineage of realized ones who show the way.
Salutations to my parents and my ancestors: may I fulfill their prayers and expectations.
Salutations to the Hindu community of Augusta, Georgia.
Salutations to Jessica, Atticus, Oscar, and Tallulah: may this little book show you what I was thinking.

1

Ganesha of Newark Avenue: An Autobiographical Introduction

Lord Ganesha came into my life at a time when I had a variety of joys and stresses. I was flat broke but also dating the woman I would eventually marry. I can place the date to sometime in 2004, when a roommate and friend of mine named Michael returned from a trip to India. He was a seminarian, and I was a graduate student at Drew University in Madison, New Jersey. We lived in a houseful of five people, sharing a duplex in South Orange, New Jersey, situated halfway between our suburban campus and New York City. I had studied yoga and Vedanta at the Sivananda Centers, and had read the *Bhagavad Gita* and the *Upanishads* at odd intervals over the preceding years. Beyond that, I had no contact with devotional Hinduism outside of a few visits with my friend, Dave Buchta, to the Hare Krishna temple on Ponce De Leon in Atlanta during my time in college at Emory University. Years later in New Jersey, Michael brought home a small Ganesha *murthi*, or idol, which he placed on a small shelf next to his vestments, as he was training to become an Anglican priest. He also told stories of communities in India where the gods were worshipped side-by-side with Jesus. I felt something when I saw that elephant-headed deity sitting on a shelf. I felt a twinge of something: was it jealousy? Longing would really be too strong a word. I'll call it a spark, something similar to what I felt when I saw an image of Saint Francis passing a reed to Clare at the Cloisters Museum in New York City that led me to join the Order of Ecumenical Franciscans, a lay renewal movement. My teacher and mentor from seminary (I made a pass through the ministry for a few years), Brian Mahan, would have called it an "epiphany of recruitment," an experience that occasions a spiritual and ethical change. Mahan drew greatly from William James, who wrote extensively about conversion in the *Varieties of Religious Experience.* James saw conversion as some peripheral concern moving towards the center, an off-hand interest taking a central role in the life of the seeker.

However this encounter might be interpreted—certainly conversion would be a little strong of a word at this point—I knew I had to have such an idol for myself, and I purchased one a few days later on Newark Avenue in Jersey City. I scraped a very modest living out of teaching philosophy and civilizations courses as an adjunct at New Jersey City University. The campus is situated in what amounts to a sixth borough of New York, a dense, diverse urban area right across the Hudson from Manhattan. Every day on my way home from work, I drove down Newark Avenue to get back on the Newark Turnpike to take me to South Orange. I had a few seconds of India each day before entering the maze of rusting steel and shipping containers that led to the Oranges. On Newark Avenue, storefronts displayed gold jewelry fit for Sita or Lakshmi, a variety of fruit and dry goods with a sub-continental emphasis, and, my personal favorite, restaurants and food stands with loads of vegetarian delights (I had been vegetarian off and on since the age of 16, and this played no small part in my attraction to things Indian). Sometimes I would get a *masala dosa* (a delicious crispy pancake filled with spiced potatoes) after teaching particularly stressful classes and take it home in a Styrofoam container, or, if I was feeling particularly indulgent, would eat it right in the car, staining my fingers yellow with turmeric. I knew that I could find a *murthi* somewhere on Newark Avenue, and saw a perfect resin image of Ganesha seated on a lotus in a jewelry shop just a minute after parking my car. I asked the price, and the shopkeeper said, "five… no eight dollars." I knew that I could have haggled but did not, and, within a half hour, Ganesha was seated on my desk, atop the CPU of my rather dated computer.

I worked pretty often on my doctoral dissertation on French philosopher Maurice Merleau-Ponty at that desk, which I had purchased secondhand, and it was cluttered with books and papers. I didn't think much about the *murthi* but viewed it as a sort of good luck charm, which, of course it is. It would be many more years before I realized its deep spiritual and philosophical significance, which I do not pretend to understand fully even now. The idol traveled with me to Georgia after my wife got a job down south, and I replaced it in its old position on my computer. As I worked on the dissertation, I began making frequent prayers to Lord Ganesha to speed the writing process, to keep me from losing references, to help me get a job. These were deeply practical prayers, far removed from the silent mysticism I had experienced as a retreatant in a Trappist monastery earlier in my youth. And yet these were prayers, too, selfish though they might have been. I made Ganesha a promise, that if my dissertation were completed and published as a book, I would write a book about him as well. Now that he has kept up his end of the bargain and much more, I belatedly and not without trepidation find time to dedicate a book to the beloved elephant-headed deity.

Through the teachings of the Himalayan Academy in Hawaii, I became acquainted with a simple Ganesh puja liturgy. It could be performed in under thirty minutes and contained all of the elements of a typical Hindu prayer service: the offering of fire, water, flame, incense, flowers, and food to the deity, who is held to be present at the ritual in a subtle or etheric form. The prayers were written in their Sanskrit form in the Devanagari script, in an English transliteration, and in English translation. I could recite the prayers in Sanskrit while also understanding their meaning. Now I came to not just be the possessor of a good luck charm but the devotee of a God with a well-developed popular and scholarly theology. Several things impressed me about the *puja* (a word for worship that literally means "acquisition of merit). The ritual had a very intimate and sensual dimension through the use of the material elements. Lighting the *deepa* (lamp) and the incense, offering cut flowers and sweets, washing and dressing the image, all had the effect of harnessing my senses towards spiritual purposes. I didn't have to work hard to concentrate, because the ritual actions themselves held my attention naturally, as a prayer in physical form. Now I could worship at my own discretion, and my whole body was integrated into the effort.

The associations or qualities of Lord Ganesha also fulfilled a spiritual need that had troubled my religious life for some time. As a Christian, I always felt a deep divide between the spiritual and the earthly. My prayer life and my practical life mixed together like oil and water, which is to say, not at all. I always felt a keen sense of competition between what I saw as my obedience to God and my earthly duties. When I read about "Christian freedom" in various pious works, I did not understand the meaning of the phrase. I had to neglect family, schoolwork, or paid occupation in order to serve God through prayer: my image of God was one of a rigid and ever-present taskmaster. I found none of that in the Ganesha puja liturgy: here was a god in which the practical and spiritual completely coincided: the one hundred and eight names of Ganesha included elements that might be considered mundane or earthly alongside others that pointed to the transcendent and heavenly. Here I found a ritualized expression of the philosophy propounded in the *Bhagavad Gita*: fulfilling the daily duties of life became an expression of devotion. I brought my thoughts and worries about work, home, and money into worship and left them there. Similarly, the fragrant scent of sandalwood suffused my entire life, and I saw the divine fire in the people and things I encountered.

The Ganesh puja opened new pathways for spirituality in my life. I became acquainted with the Shiva Puja with the help of a local temple community, and I also learned prayers to Shri Lakshmi. After falling away from the Christian ministry (a long story for another time), my devotional life became stronger, and I filled spare minutes with *japa* (saying the names of God), *kirtan* (singing holy songs), *puja* (ritualized worship), and *dhyana* (philosophical contemplation of the divine). Opening the door to God with the Ganesha puja led to many other openings, many transformations that reverberated throughout my life. Those acquainted with the elephant-headed deity often say that he is the easiest God to encounter, and I have found that to be true. The simple elements of the puja and the prayers that go along with them led me to a state of peace that would have taken hours or days to achieve through silent meditation. By the time I got to the 108 names of Ganesha in the liturgy, I felt like I had encountered him in the flesh on Mount Kailas itself. I could hear the sounds of his drumming in my mind, and my life oriented itself to his rhythms.

There are many stories of the birth of Lord Ganesh in the *Puranas,* which are supplementary texts to the *Vedas,* but they all agree that Ganesh is the deity to be propitiated first, the God of new beginnings. It is customary in India and throughout the world—wherever followers of the Sanatana Dharma can be found—to worship the Remover of Obstacles before any new undertaking, whether before getting married, starting a business, or simply heading out of the house for the day. The Romans had a similar tradition in the two-headed deity, Janus, the God of the threshold. The Romans placed an image of Janus over doorways, and they said prayers to Janus at the beginning of the day and at any important transition in life. Ganesh plays the same role, but, unlike the case of Janus, his cult still lives in the hearts of over a billion devotees. Some of the world's wealthiest people and the world's poorest people have a shrine tucked away in an honored place: they all hope for spiritual and material comfort, for the light of true wisdom in a dark world. I know that they find it, when they worship with sincerity and faith.

Some iconography and mythic traditions associate Ganesh with his two "wives," *riddhi* (prosperity) and *siddhi* (spiritual power or attainment). Many devotees pray to Ganesh or Lakshmi with the straightforward intention of gaining material wealth. This might come across as obscene or shallow at first glance, but several factors should be kept in mind. First, it should be said that those who pray for material rewards because they really need them have every right to do so: no one would begrudge a poor person for praying for food or safe lodging. Next, even those who are already well-heeled and yet still pray for material gain may experience a transformation by turning to Lord Ganesh. Worship makes the devotee more cognizant of the wealth all around us: the beauty of the natural world, the joys of family and home, the privilege of honorable work, and the presence of realized teachers among us. The desire for wealth becomes a pathway to the divine, a way for God to speak to human beings. Hinduism teaches that nothing good can come of suppressing desire, for we all get to union with God eventually. The same might be said of the desire for *siddhis*, supernatural powers. As a child and into adulthood, I was fascinated with ESP, astral projection, and other paranormal topics, and this interest eventually led to more traditional Christian and Hindu devotional practices. Someone may come to Lord Ganesha's feet hoping to gain some supernatural ability: whether they find it or not will not matter in the end, because Lord Ganesha's loving presence will be enough.

The fact remains that no one comes to spiritual practices with completely pure intentions—that comes after the fact and not before. Like someone piloting a hot air balloon, the spiritual aspirant (*sadhak*) tosses off the sand bags one by one, until only silence remains. The "sand bags" in this case are the errant thoughts that constantly trouble the mind: the infinite worries that inevitably arise in material life. Roughly speaking, the difference between Hindu devotional practices and other traditions like Zen Buddhism and philosophical Taoism is that Hindus believe that they can enter into the more perfect meditation of the gurus and the *devas*. *Puja* establishes a link between the gross, subtle, and spiritual worlds, so that the devotee benefits from the greater peace and tranquility of those who have gone before. Human beings and gods differ not in kind, but in the degree of attainment, and human beings can become divine with sufficient practice. Paraphrasing a prayer to Shiva in the more ancient form of Rudra, the *Rudrashtadhyayi,* the deities help to cast off a sluggish state of mind and attain greater degrees of spiritual perfection. Most iconography of the gods includes weapons: in Ganesha's case often an axe (more on the imagery later), which provokes this warrior-like mentality. Every ounce of effort must be summoned in the fight against negative states of mind like anger, resentment, sadness, jealousy, and greed.

This points to the chief difference between Hindu and Christian theology. Most observers would say that the greatest differences exist in the propitiation of idols and in the proliferation of divine forms, but the doctrine of the Trinity already suggests a plurality-in-unity; so much ground for dialogue between the faiths already exists there. Beyond the outward forms of worship, a greater theological difference would arise over the doctrine of original sin, which holds that no human being, apart from Jesus, can ever enter into moral or spiritual perfection. I do not wish to quibble over such matters in a dry, academic way: I only raise the point to say that this particular doctrine can and does discourage spiritual effort in many Christians. Hinduism holds the door to divinity open wider, saying that anyone can attain perfection, which leads to the proliferation of forms and the remarkable elasticity and vibrancy of the faith. American- and European-dwelling Hindus do not have the same degree of spirituality penetrating daily life: gone here are the village shrines, the sacred trees, the thousands of temples, the enormous festivals that can be found in India. Still, the same mindset prevails, which sees in the light glinting off leaves the smile of a goddess, which finds in an unexpected visit from a friend the presence of a god, which sees in flame, water, flowers, and incense a portal to heaven. No faith on earth has such a vast and complicated body of scripture and mythology, and yet, in the elements of a simple *puja* can be found a highly efficient means to access greater peace and joy.

Such a ritual can last for days or even years, or it can take place in the few minutes before a morning commute. Either way, this human world becomes a little more humane, a little slower and more reflective, a little more open to kindliness and charity. People of many backgrounds, atheist, pagan, Christian, Muslim, Jewish, Sikh, and "none of the above," will appreciate the good qualities that Ganesh devotion instills. In the words of Socrates in the *Apology*, "Is there anyone who would rather be harmed than benefited?" In this spirit, we should hope that the devotional life does not run dry, because, without it, the world would be a less tolerable place to live. I know that many thinkers reach quite the opposite conclusion—that religion makes people more hateful and intolerant. Every faith has its extremes, but I believe that, when kept to its rudiments of peace and compassion, devotional practices really do make people more mindful of others than themselves, more accepting of the world as it is rather than as they would like it to be, and more likely to see in the face of the stranger a manifestation of the divine. It is harder to harm someone who you think is a god in disguise, and, for this reason, we do well to hearken to traditional practices from around the world that give us the eyes to see this innate divinity.

I have strayed pretty far from Newark Avenue at this point, and the first Ganesh idol that I purchased there. Eventually I moved that image to my office (when I finally had a full-time university job), where it still sits on a low, narrow windowsill afforded by the 1970s era architecture of my building. It has clothes now, as I sewed it some outfits, tiny *dhotis*, in various colors with a golden ribbon for fringe. I taped a poster triptych of Ganesh, Shiva, and Murugan (or Karttikeya, Ganesha's brother) just above it, along with a devotional card of the Virgin Mary from my days of Catholic exploration. Above that, I have an AUM sun-catcher in my window that complements nicely the holly tree outside. I say prayers in my office at odd intervals, and, so far, no one has complained about the chanting that I sometimes do aloud. Classes and writing go better when I stay on top of my spiritual game, and I feel happy knowing that I am progressing towards a greater goal than tenure, though that milestone, too, came and went. Problems slough off my back more easily when devotion ebbs, and water cooler grumbling becomes less contagious. My anti-social self has become more open to others, and my otherworldliness has learned to bend down and touch the soil. I have become more of a monotheist and yet more of a pagan at the same time.

For my home, I purchased a larger bronze image of dancing Ganesha, that speaks to me of good timing, another one of Ganapati's attributes. He holds the *damaru* (the drum of creation), in one hand and is captured mid-step, twirling in motion like his father, Shiva, whose dance sustains and destroys the universe. The image reminds me of the counsel of the *Bhagavad Gita* to avoid attachment to action but also to avoid attachment to inaction. "Keep things moving," Ganesha says to me, "Work on your projects, maintain your household, and say your prayers. Leave the rest up to me." This image is installed in a German silver shrine above the fireplace of our small, postwar ranch house in the busy living room where our children play and our dog lounges. I am reminded of a phrase from Plotinus, which I paraphrase as "Being-heart-hearth-home": the hearth is the heart of the home, just as Being lies at the heart of all things. If I can remember that sacred fire, Agni, at all times, then I will see the true, blazing nature of reality, stripped of its veil of mundane existence. Give me not only the surfaces of things, but the surfaces as lit from within, by the radiance of the divine. Some would call this kind of talk romanticism or fantasy, but those who know see it as a straightforward description of the world as it is. Our frenetic lifestyles make the world appear to be dull, so that we have to seek fantasy in various forms of entertainment. For those who can truly see, those whom Plotinus calls the Proficient, watching the grass grow can be truly exhilarating. The approach towards sight requires silent effort, what I have called the "labor of attention," but, for those who are willing to work, great rewards await.

The gods will not make the effort for us: those who want to live as mystics in a world of consumers definitely have an uphill battle. But the gods can make the journey more enjoyable: they can be companions on the road and a great encouragement. We should also keep in mind always that they do not represent something separate from ourselves, aristocrats to whom we must beg for alms. Rather, the gods represent the latent powers within ourselves; aspects of our true nature. The word "represent" should not be taken in any way as a slight: the idol in the shrine prefigures something real. We show the *murthi* devotion, because it makes manifest in the world of "objects and relationships" what otherwise could not be seen by the eye. We learn to augment the physical eyes with the third eye of insight, which sees everything as God. Call it pantheism, panentheism, animism, or even monotheism—the labels don't matter—only see the More to the world that goes unnoticed most of the time. We don't see the More, because we concentrate on less. Attention diverted to this or that cannot be devoted to That. Time must be taken, stolen for spiritual practice, otherwise vitality leaks out of our lives and we cling to distraction out of desperation.

But I never finished the story of the dancing Ganesha. I found this new idol beautiful, but I had developed an attachment to the old one, because it had been with me for so long. The little image from Newark Avenue had an upraised fist (*mushti mudra*), which suggested Ganesh saying, "I've got this under control." The new idol, fresh out of packing peanuts, still felt like a normal object. I knew that there must be some prayer to install a new deity in a shrine, so I started looking for one on the internet. I found that most people don't say a formal prayer to install the deity other than the typical daily prayers, but there is a prayer to be had. It's called *prana pratishta,* the establishment of life. *Prana* is the Sanskrit word for what Taoists might call *chi,* the hidden life-force that flows through all things, even things like stones that we have been trained to think are dead. The prayer makes the statue into a *murthi,* transforms it from a work of art to a living thing. I obtained the prayer from Swami Satyananda Saraswati, who expounds the *shakti* teachings of Shree Maa of Kamakhya, who is, in turn, a direct disciple of Shri Ramakrishna and Sarada Maa. In a few short months, I became a devotee of Swamiji and Shree Maa, but it all started with the dancing Ganesha.

I had tried to contact other spiritual teachers before. One American guru who carries himself in a very traditional, Indian fashion never responded to any of my queries. Other teachers corresponded only through their devotees and never answered any inquiries directly. I found none of this with Swamiji. He answered my questions in a simple and straightforward way without delay, giving me the answer to my question and nothing more. There was no self-aggrandizing or standing on principle: just someone who genuinely cared about transmitting the teachings. His method of conducting himself already taught me a lot about how to work efficiently, lessons that I am still learning. I said the appropriate prayer and began worshipping the new image, and later I read the *Guru Gita,* a scripture to which Swamiji referred me. The *Guru Gita* identifies the guru with Shiva himself and promises a more direct path to the divine through selfless service of the respected "remover of darkness." It took many months of study for the scripture to take root in me.

I regarded it as interesting, perhaps even profound, but it did not mean much to me personally. I appreciated the guru principle as a concept, but it had no effect on my life. All the time I knew the value of a true teacher, and I asked Ganesha daily to reveal my teacher to me.

At the same time, the *sadhana* prescribed to me by Swamiji had already begun to take effect: I chanted the 1000 names of Kali each week, and a few of them particularly spoke to me. Kali, the great remover of darkness, destroyer of the armies of thought, also had these names which spoke directly to my heart: "paramā-nandabhairav," in Swamiji's translation, "She Who is the Supreme Bliss Beyond All Fear (753); "tarunabhairav," or "She Who is the Energy that Pulls Beyond Fear" (757); or, more emphatically, "narakāntakā," "She Who is the End of All Hell"(619)! I had many fears, an army of fears, most of them tied to memories of the past and not worth repeating. Mostly I didn't want to fail, to go down a spiritual path that would lead nowhere, to waste precious time and effort with an unfamiliar spiritual tradition. I worried about stories of false gurus who rob their disciples of wealth while contributing nothing to their development as people. These prayers assuaged my doubts and gave me courage that the Divine Mother herself would see my aspirations to satisfaction, that I had found, at last, the right path. Hell had been the endless delay, the years of seeking and not finding: liberation would be sitting at the feet of a true Master, as I had sat at the foot of my Ganesha idol.

Having a living preceptor did not change my life overnight: I still had bills to pay, children to raise, and a university job. Some things did change, though: I learned the meanings of seed (*bija*) mantras that previously made no sense to me. I became acquainted with more prayers and pujas: a goddess-based prayer known as the *Chandi*, the Indra-themed puja known as *Rudrastadyayai*, the Hanuman *Chalisa*, and a longer form of the Śiva puja. These prayers became a sacred thread running through my life, an imperishable chain making temporal life more serene and enjoyable. I learned to make the journey into worship and carry some of that worship back with me into the world, and I learned to recognize the divine presence in the midst of everyday life. My devotion still had waxing and waning cycles, but these were not as erratic as before. I could regain my focus a little more easily and gain concentration with less effort. I had moments of brilliant clarity, where I saw all of the "good" and "bad" aspects of life as aspects of the divine play.

In January of 2012, Swamiji bestowed upon me the spiritual name Janyananda Saraswati: Janya is pronounced more like John—John-ya. Swamiji translates Janyananda as "Who is One with All Beings Born," which felt appropriate to me as a philosopher who studies animal and environmental ethics. I thought that the name of the tribe of Saraswati fit my vocation as well, since she is the goddess of learning and wisdom. Hindu families also have a *gotra*, or guru lineage, and Swamiji adopted me into the Satyananda *gotra*, named after the guru of King Janak, who was the first guru of our lineage and the father of Sita, Lord Ram's consort and an avatara of Shri Lakshmi. Swamiji authorized me to consecrate a sacred thread and perform the *upanayanam* rite. The thread has many layers of meanings and associations, like most things in Sanatana Dharma, but most basically represents the Gayatri mantra, which the wearer pledges to say at least three times a day for life. Every Hindu knows the Gayatri mantra, which is entoned, *"om bhur bhuvah svahah/tat savitur varenyam/bhargo devasya dhimahi/dhyo yo na prachodayat."* I have read many translations, all of which differ and are nonetheless correct in picking up the shades of association in the Sanskrit. The prayer means approximately "Om the gross world, the subtle world, the divine world. May that Savitur light give increase to our meditations." The prayer, symbolized by the thread looped around three times and tied securely, binds together the physical world, the world of thoughts or mind, and the world of the *devas* or energy. Other threefold associations include purity in thought, word, and deed or the binding of the three gunas (qualities in nature) of *rajas* (activity), *tamas* (inertia), and *sattva* (clarity).[1] While the thread, called *yajnopavita* in Sanskrit, is nothing more than spun cotton in a material sense, it represents an armor composed of energetic mantras with which it is invested and maintained. Just as the tantric devotee places mantras on the parts of the body, the sacred thread is a garland of energy that encircles the wearer at all times, from the moment of investiture until death.

Have I reached Enlightenment? Well, I have come to regard that question, itself, as rather illusory. "Enlightenments" would be a better way of saying it, with emphasis on the *plural*, rather than the capital letter. Swamiji says that there are many initiations into yoga, many deepenings, many revelations: in fact, they are inexhaustible. To reach "Enlightenment" would be a bit sad, for it would mean the end of a beautiful, albeit sometimes painful and sorrowful journey. I can say that I have found tools to lighten the load, to help me to see more clearly, to stay on the good side of life. I don't mean this in the sometimes trite sense of "positive thinking," but in seeing the *negatives themselves* as part of the journey towards liberation. Swamiji and Shree Maa have taught me to keep going, to keep serving, to keep practicing, and to find stillness in this perpetual movement. To dance with Ganesha is to forever expand one's sense of possibility, to push oneself ever closer to the divine nature as it unfolds in this world. Eventually we come to regard ourselves not as separate beings, but as aspects of Ganesha's nature. We come to be the removers of obstacles for others. We accept his hospitality so that we can offer that hospitality to others. We keep the shrine of worship clean so that we can keep the shrine of the heart clean. And in this way the dance of mutuality continues, encompassing people, earth, animals, gods, spirits, and ancestors. The path forward for humanity, the only way that does not lead to destruction, lies in mutual service and submission. Ganesha, with his playful, happy spirit, can be a good model for the interior attitude that must be adopted in order for this new vision to emerge.

Although I have had my fair share of education, mostly in Western philosophy and theology, I speak in these pages as a devotee and not as a pundit or theologian. I will try to avoid the "Westerner who appropriates Eastern religion" stereotype, as I present the worship of the elephant-faced deity in a way that I believe is faithful to Indian teachings. If Westerners have converted Hindus to Christianity for all of these centuries of colonialism and globalization, isn't it only fair that a few of those conversions should go the other way? Any faults in this book certainly lie with myself and not with any of my teachers or associates. As for Lord Ganesha, he can handle anything that I might say about him, as the Lord is much more forgiving and understanding than any human being. Devotion teaches everything to the true seeker, and without it, no one advances at all in true spiritual understanding. I am not worried about the future of Sanatana Dharma, otherwise known as Hinduism, as the truth has a way of perpetuating itself without violence or compulsion. The best way to preserve the teachings, the best way to advance the Dharma, is to practice it. I hope that this book will inspire and enable that practice.

II

Christianity and Hinduism: Opposites or Complements?

Almost every major Hindu saint has at some time read and appreciated the teachings of Jesus, and many authors have seen Jesus as a great yogi. Christian writers have also studied and appreciated Hinduism, although in a more cautious and qualified way. I would like to suggest that Ganapati, in his capacity as the guardian of the gateway, can open the doors between these two traditions, breaking down the obstacles to greater understanding. By speaking here only of Christianity and Hinduism, I do not mean to exclude other faiths. I am speaking here as someone who happens to have the most experience with these two traditions: in Christianity as a Protestant seminarian and rural minister, and, in Hinduism, as a lay follower of a Shakti lineage descended from Shri Ramakrishna (although my teachers hesitate to use designations like "Shakti," "Vaishnava," "Shaivite," and the like). I contend that much of what I say here could be applied to other traditions, but I will leave it to others to make these connections.

It should first be noticed that Christianity and Hinduism have a great path to conversation in the doctrine of the Trinity, which acknowledges a plurality in the divine nature. The American philosopher Charles Sanders Peirce said that all numbers are implied in the number three, since three-ness breaks out of both duality and monism. Readers of the book of Genesis will remember the royal "we" of the first creation story, "Let *us* make humankind in *our* own image..." Hindus take the divine multiplicity farther than Christians, ultimately saying, "what difference does it make whether we speak of three or three-hundred thirty million?" And, of course, Hinduism has many Trinitarian formulations: think of Brahma, Vishnu, and Shiva, the creator, preserver, and destroyer. My own shakti tradition worships these three divine persons along with their feminine counterparts, Saraswati, Lakshmi, and Sita, in the Cosmic Puja. Just as Christians worship not one-third of God's being when they worship Jesus, but the entirety of the divine nature, in the same way Hindus worship the entirety of the divine nature when they worship Ganesh or Rama or Śiva. So Ganesh is called "Ganapati," the lord of the *ganas*, or divine attendants, but Śiva also goes by the same title. Innumerable examples could be given of this divine interpenetration. So these divine incarnations or faces of the divine, "prosopon" is the term the Greek fathers used, highlight different aspects of divinity, but they are all equally pathways to God. At a street-level of understanding, we pray to Lakshmi for wealth and Saraswati for wisdom, but, at a deeper level of devotion, these two goddesses are but two different entrances to the house of divine knowledge.

The similarities between the two traditions (actually thousands of distinct traditions, gathered under the umbrella terms, "Christianity," and "Hinduism") do not stop there. Jesus says in John 10:16, "I have other sheep that do not belong to this fold," implying that those who listen to his message will extend beyond the bounds of his immediate disciples. Anyone who believes in nonviolence and in concern for the poor and the created order implicitly believes in the teachings of Jesus. The passage most often used to beat non-Christians over the head actually gains a different meaning when read in the light of Sanatana Dharma. I refer to a passage a few chapters later in John, which reads, "I am the way, the truth, and the life. No one comes to the Father except through me" (14:16). Jesus here expounds nothing other than the guru principle. The audience for this message is, of course, the disciples in the upper room, where they have gathered for a final meal before the death of Jesus. This message is not intended as some sort of blanket condemnation of non-Christians (more properly, non-Jews, for

Christianity hadn't been invented yet!), but rather says that for those who have been touched by Jesus, he remains the way to salvation. Hindus affirm the same thing when they say that those who have taken initiation from a particular guru should remain with that guru rather than continuing to "shop around" in the marketplace of religious ideas. When Jesus says "I am the way," he is saying that he has become so identified with God that there is no longer any separation between himself and the divine. Hinduism aims at this same exact goal, but it refuses to say that only one person in all of history can ever achieve it.

The doctrine of original sin in Christianity has always been troubling to me, for how could the regeneration in Christ ever take effect if original sin presented a permanent limit of advance? The saints of the Orthodox and Roman Catholic traditions offered a bit of respite from what I saw as the mediocrity of the Protestant traditions: saved from hell but never fully 'cured' of the 'disease' of sin. I wanted what John Wesley called "entire sanctification" and not just a sort of symbolic covering of sin or a vicarious or sacrificial atonement. I wanted to become a complete person in the real world and not just on the metaphysical level: if it couldn't affect the way I lived my life, I wasn't interested. A couple of key texts made the transition to Hinduism more natural: *The Way of a Pilgrim,* which outlined the hesychastic path of continual repetition of the Jesus Prayer, which sounded to me rather like the practice of *nama japa* in Hinduism. This I supplemented with a volume of the *Little Russian Philokalia,* a book on hesychasm recommended by some Orthodox monks I encountered in Northwest Georgia. Another key book was the *Practice of the Presence of God* by Brother Lawrence, which also recommended an interior beseeching of the divine presence in daily life. I read these little gems not as academic treatises but as instruction manuals, and I found that they certainly worked. While not practicing hesychastic devotion, however, I returned to the rather Protestant practice of spiritual journaling, which basically meant keeping a daily record of my sins and shortcomings and focusing on ways to enact some sort of spiritual revolution that always remained on the horizon but never arrived.

I learned that some heterodox groups did not espouse or downplayed the doctrine of original sin: I am thinking of Rastafarianism and a contemporary movement little known in the church called *A Course in Miracles*. Then I was also familiar with ancient Gnosticism from my church history courses, especially a text called the *Hymn of the Pearl*, which had a view of salvation similar to Platonic recollection. Another way, which I felt could also be justified through scripture, seemed to say that we all have a divine nature that has been obscured through disuse. On this interpretation, Jesus becomes the Christ through adoption, and the title, "Son of God," points to the justice and mercy of Christ rather than his absolute uniqueness. On this interpretation, we can all become sons and daughters of God through prayer and good works, and this seemed to square with what I read in the gospels. After all, Jesus said that his followers would do even greater things than he did (John 14:12), and Saint Paul said that Jesus would be the first of many brothers (Romans 8:29). I began to imagine that perhaps doctrines of "total depravity," in the Calvinist language, had departed from the meaning of the gospels, which were supposed to be good news. I could not see how perpetual sinfulness could ever be good, and the more vicarious theories of the atonement didn't resolve the difficulty for me.

Another Christian idea, also derived from Paul, troubled me, and that was the idea of the church as the body of Christ (1 Corinthians 12:27). I grew up in the church as the son of two ministers, and I knew too much about the church to ever regard it as having very much to do with Christ. Without going on a tirade about the innumerable ways that the church seemed to conspire in shooing me out the door, it suffices to say that the doctrine of the church as the body of Christ tends to provide cover for a variety of less-than-optimal institutional practices. To be fair to Christian teaching, the doctrine should appropriately be taken as a mystery, akin to the "twilight language" of the tantric texts, in which contradictory ideas are juxtaposed in order to move the practitioner beyond propositional logic, as Constantina Rhodes explains in *Invoking Lakshmi*. More often than not, the church uses the "body of Christ" talk in order to silence dissent: if anyone disagrees, the thinking goes, something must be wrong with their faith. But then the church has always had a basically exclusionary practice of excluding heretics, a practice which has its roots in the Hebrew scriptures, where one holy and chosen people rejects and condemns those who belong to other systems of belief. I found myself wondering how many good Christians were condemned and burned as heretics because of some minor theological controversy that Christians today don't even understand.

I have come to believe that a monotheistic deity is just a blurred pantheon, so Yahweh is probably a Canaanite sky-god, a king of the gods, like Zeus, who gradually took over the functions of his cohorts. The epithets "King of Kings" and "Lord of Lords," as applied to Yahweh or Jesus can be found in the name recitations of many Hindu deities. Interestingly enough, the names and mythology of deities from Lithuania to Ireland can be traced back to their roots in Sanskrit, which is the grandfather tongue of both European and Slavic languages.[2] One could say that perhaps monotheism began with polytheism or henotheism but evolved beyond these older belief systems. Oftentimes, monotheistic religions (or Trinitarian, as the case may be) claim even a moral superiority to other religions, upholding the Decalogue as a case in point. But the connection between theology and ethics needs to be made more clearly, as the biblical God enjoined His followers to many atrocities in the name of the Oneness of the divine nature. The Greeks were smart enough to uphold both the One *and* the Many, which prevents the totalizing discourse of monotheism and its "convert or die" mentality. Hinduism does not securely rest on any one theological foundation and can be called by turns animistic, pantheistic, henotheistic, monotheistic, or even atheistic. This flexibility should not be regarded as a failure to develop a unified theology (for such attempts end in violence) but as the expression of a vital and living faith which cannot be confined to a single creed. Hinduism appealed to me, because it is an open source religion: no central authority gets to decide who can call themselves Hindu and who cannot. To be sure, there are orthodoxies within various Indian religious communities, but the sheer plurality of lineages prevents some hardening along doctrinal lines. Each guru chooses who to name as a successor, and some gurus, even highly saintly ones like Ramana Maharshi, do not name a successor at all but choose to let the teachings stand on their own.

Suppose a handyman used only a hammer: a hammer to fix the pipes, a hammer to re-wire the house, a hammer to fix the car. Offered a pair of pliers, some screwdrivers, and a socket wrench, it would be silly if the handyman said, "No thanks! I already have a hammer: the only tool I ever need!" Hindus view the many gods as tools in the kit: aspects of the divine nature that the devotee wants to emphasize in his or her own life. Having only one God would be like having only a hammer: useful in some respects but too crude for the fine work of living. The Oneness of God also tends to contradict the goodness of the world and all its messiness, which will not easily assimilate into this aloof God who will not consent to be a mere deity. Hindus likewise have no trouble with the term "idolatry," for they simply disagree that making images of God should be forbidden. The mind operates according to name and form: in order to go beyond the mind, one must first go as far as the mind will allow within name and form. This means worshipping an internal or external image which can only be transcended in the depths of meditation. Simply getting rid of the idol doesn't get rid of image-making, as there are plenty of images in the parables of Jesus or the verses of the Qur'an. Thinking of God as father or simply as God already amounts to image-making, commits one to a certain vision of the divine. Hindus worship now Ram, now Lakshmi, now Shiva, but they insist that these permutations are all correct ways to envision God, like turning a cut gemstone to see all of its different facets.

I don't mean to multiply divisions here or to imply the superiority the Hindu way: readers can easily find that kind of talk elsewhere. I only want to share something of the way that I came to this path so that others who have had similar experiences will be able to follow my trail of breadcrumbs. Shree Maa teaches that God resides in every atom of this great universe, and theological disputes dissolve easily in hearts softened by the interior experience of awakening. Everyone has had touches of bliss in life, moments of genuine joy, and spiritual practices at their best make this lightheartedness more easily available. When religion divides people, something has gone horribly wrong, for the goal of the world's faiths should be to make us loving servants of each other and servants of the earth and animals. We all fall short of this from time to time, and the ritual practices bring us back to square one, so that we can start anew. The forms of the gods belong to the remote ancestry of humankind, and yet they glisten anew each day, each day the old songs ring in human hearts. The cymbals chime, and the drums beat. The smoke from the sacred fire rises, and the chanting begins. We have the option to pretend we don't hear, or we can join in the refrain. For my part, I would rather invite the old songs into my heart, for they banish the gloom of my solitary existence and open my eyes to a world of vibrant life.

III

Iconography of Lord Ganesha

Ankusha: The Goad

Lord Ganesha is depicted holding a goad in one of his hands. Used by mahouts, or elephant drivers, the goad provokes the elephant, the world's largest land animal, into doing what the driver wants. Contrary to expectations, elephants have very sensitive skin, and the hook can be driven lightly or severely into the elephant to provoke pain. Ganesha, the divine being represented as part elephant, holds his own goad, which is to say that he has no driver other than his own nature. He needs no external motivation to do as he wills but has fully mastered his own faculties.

The implications for meditation and the spiritual life are clear. Lord Ganesha will not prod his devotees with the goad unless they contemplate his nature as the self-gathered one, the one who has control of all desires, who understands and can control his own motivations. For those who truly seek his guidance, who have so purified their minds as to understand themselves, Ganesh will occasionally prod them to undertake some neglected task or discover a new venture. Those who feel the nudging of ankusha, a holy pain, should consider themselves fortunate indeed, for this indicates that progress has been made on the spiritual path.

The goad may also indicate stubbornness in those who are refusing to listen to some guidance or piece of wisdom. It should remind us to listen most deeply for the divine and to those who care about our well-being. We should develop that thick skin that looks tough from the outside but is nonetheless very sensitive: plowing through obstacles and yet, at the same time, alert to any contingencies that may arise in a given situation. We should seek to be pained when we should be pained, to be appropriately regretful when we have done something wrong, to allow that sting of conscience to propel us into more appropriate action.

Modaka: The Bowl of Sweets

Ganesh is a great yogi, the embodiment and manifestation of his father Shiva's asceticism. And yet Ganesh often appears dancing or with a quite joyful expression on his face. He is *lambodaraya,* the one with a round belly, and he holds a bowlful of sweets. This aspect of his iconography means that Ganesh has not forgotten how to laugh and have a good time. He is not like some dour-faced saints in various religious traditions who are moral scolds and spend their time only in reflection on death. Shri Ganesha is free from all attachment, and this freedom allows him to indulge in the joys of life without clinging to them.

The modaka balls that he holds are often prepared at festival times in India, and therefore, represent the joys of family and community as well as prosperity in general. He holds them out, as if offering them to his devotees even as they offer sweets to him. This joyful interchange between humans and the devas (the gods or immortals) is the fountain of bliss at the center of existence. As we serve each other and share with each other, we increase the joy available in the world.

The bowl of sweets reminds us to give thanks for what we have, to share with others, and to not take ourselves too seriously in the religious life. Of course, the sweets also taste good, and they remind us that our physical bodies, too, are important. We remember that *kama,* pleasure, and *artha,* wealth, are two of the four aims of life. When used appropriately, that is, when contained, just as the modaka are contained in the bowl, these blessings of life can bring great joy. When selfishly hoarded or obtained unethically, they produce suffering in ourselves and others.

The Noose

The noose restrains devotees from undertaking adharmic action that would hinder the further development of that individual in that incarnation. This action of Lord Ganesha is extremely subtle and can only be experienced by advanced practitioners who have spent a great deal of time in silent meditation, in addition to the more outward forms of devotion found in worship and scriptural study. The noose reminds me of Socrates' divine sign, which he described during his trial in Athens. The divine sign seems to have been a kind of voice which never told the barefoot, aged philosopher what to do but simply restrained him when he contemplated doing something wrong. The same thing happens to serious devotees of Lord Ganesha, who may feel that sense of inner restraint when something threatens to disturb the inner stillness or sense of peace. In order for the noose to be felt, one must first actively want to live the disciplined life. Think of it not as form of violent coercion—it's not a hangman's noose—but as a form of guidance or tutelage. Use the vehicle of this incarnation to move closer to the goal of liberation, and think of every circumstance that arises as part of a training program that leads to the goal.

The Axe

The axe represents good actions, the ultimate weapon of the adherent of dharma. Nothing brings the individual worshipper closer to realization that undertaking the correct course of action, a topic discussed extensively in Krishna's conversation with Arjuna in the *Bhagavad Gita.* The ignorant person acts according to inclination, wandering to and fro between one desire and another, while the wise person acts according to the dictates of conscience and the call of duty to gods, ancestors, guru, family, occupation, and community. Worship bends the mind away from egotistical attachment and closer to the goal of dutiful action.

The Lotus

The lotus is a near-universal symbol of enlightenment in Asian religions. It grows in the mucky, watery places, and yet its flower emerges from the mud in pristine condition. The lotus thus stands for purity of spirit in the midst of the chaos of the world. The flower blossoms slowly over several days, unfolding gradually, petal by petal, which hints at the slow nature of spiritual progress. The flower is also a symbol of Śri Lakshmi, the goddess of good fortune, with whom Ganesha is closely associated. The quality of *śri*, the original name for the goddess, encompasses all spiritual and worldly good, and the commensurability of material and spiritual perfection. Devotees of Ganesha, like those of Lakshmi, affirm that life in the world can be reconciled with the quest for spiritual liberation. Many Hindu scriptures mention a lotus that will never lose its luster, which can be seen as a reference to the heart chakra or the crown chakra at the top of the head. Thinking about flowers that grace the altar in a home or a temple, the flowers that never lose their luster are those that are changed regularly for new flowers. What seem like the same flowers have actually been changed repeatedly by devotees. The lotus flower can be seen as a sign of the need to continually renew devotion, just as the lotus blooms anew each year. The "flowers" of the chakras are likewise opened by continual *sadhana*, spiritual practice.

Musical Instruments

Lord Ganesha is frequently depicted with musical instruments, such as *mrdanga*, *tabla*, or *damaru* drums, a harmonium, a *vina*, or cymbals. Lord Ganesha traditionally sits on the muladhara chakra at the base of the spine. This chakra is related to the incarnation as Kurma, the tortoise that supported the world as the gods churned the ocean of milk at the beginning of this cycle of ages. As the gods churn, many gifts, such as divine weapons, the kaustubha gem, and goddess Mahalakshmi herself emanate from the churning. The churning represents devotion, the pre-eminent human activity from which many gifts spring. The *dev astras*, the weapons of the gods, are good qualities, like patience, honesty, and moderation, and good actions, like giving and service. All of these actions and qualities begin with a root principle of balance and integration. Just as a tall building cannot be constructed without a good foundation, the devotional life begins with sitting. As we sit in lotus posture, half lotus, or simply in a chair, we can make that seat divine and magical by invoking the elephant-headed deity. Ganesha makes the seat good and holy by removing physical, mental, and spiritual distractions. So Ganesh helps disciples to overcome that itchy back or aching ankle, that worry or stress, or the accumulations of past karma.

As Lord of timing, Ganesha ensures that activities throughout the day align in a harmonic way, just as the musicians in an ensemble coordinate their efforts to produce a good sound, a sound in which no one plays over each other, where everyone stays on the same beat. Ganesh coordinates members of a spiritual household or business in the same manner, so that no effort is lost. Music has other aspects, in which it inspires happiness and joy in the listener. Just so, Ganesh can be seen dancing in many images, which betokens joy at the good things in life, enrapture with the divine presence, and sufficient energy devoted to the completion of a task. He does not dance half-heartedly, and his large frame nonetheless has the nimble lightness of a ballerina. Devotees come to recognize his dance steps, the footprints painted on the floor, so to speak, and harmonize their melodies with Ganapati's. This harmonization begins in the puja and radiates outward from there to the whole of life. The *damaru*, the small, handheld, double-headed drum, represents the power of creation of creation and destruction, the larger melody of the entire universe. Ganesha's father is Śiva, the cosmic meditator, who is the Consciousness of Infinite Goodness, the consciousness of everything, the consciousness of nature itself. By tuning in to the rhythms and melodies of Ganapati's dance, we align ourselves with that larger principle, the unfolding of nature. As we become aware that we, too, are but ripples in this larger pond, our egoistic attachment diminishes, along with the problems and pains that go along with the individualistic perspective.

The music of the dancing Ganesha also has its correlates in the human body, which the devotee learns to recognize through Ganesha's tutelage. The heartbeat, together with the inflowing and outflowing breath, represents the same centrifugal and centripetal force at work in the universe as a whole. This symbolism runs deeply throughout all phases of existence: from the waxing and waning of the moon to the ebb and flow of the tides to cycles of drought and flood to the changing seasons to repulsion and attraction. The divine music in the cosmos can be heard within our own bodies. After much meditation, one begins to hear the *shhhh* of blood in the ears, the *thump-thump* of the heart, and the high *eeee* sound of thought itself. Beyond this, at select moments the gods may reveal the ringing tones of the celestial music, the singing of the *gandharvas* (celestial singers, kind of like angels) and *apsaras* (celestial maidens). Indeed, the devotee has already entered the celestial retinue through the practice of devotional chanting, singing, and *japa* (recitation of divine names). The person who sings divine songs with full devotion is as dear to the gods as Śiva, Indra, or Krishna. The one who understands and repeats these names has become the Proficient, the true Brahmin, the Knower of the Divine.

The broken tusk

Legend has it that the sage, Vyāsa, revealer of the *Mahābhārata* epic, could not write down words fast enough to commit to paper the intense revelations that came into his consciousness. He appealed to Lord Brahmā, the creator and god of Wisdom, for help, and the Grandfather sent Ganesha, who was able to compose verses with all four of his hands, thus accomplishing what it would take two ambidextrous humans to achieve.[3] It is also said that he broke his tusk to hurl as a weapon or to use as a writing implement. Ganesha, also known as "ekadantaya," the one-tusked, also has other qualities associated with oneness, such as single-pointed devotion and oneness with his father, Śiva. What might be seen as a limitation or flaw—the "missing" tusk—becomes his weapon or instrument and also his calling card. The symbolism means that Ganesha takes defects and makes them into tools, thereby overcoming them. The quickness with which he fights his adversaries and composes poetry he also pours into his devotees' lives, making them quick and nimble as well.

The sugarcane bow

The sugarcane bow stands for wealth and prosperity or for increase in social standing. Sometimes the sugarcane will actually be strung like a bow in Ganesha iconography, indicating that the deva wounds his followers with the kindness of good gifts.[4] Many legends are told about the sugarcane, including one in which Lord Shiva miraculously feeds a stone image of an elephant with sugarcane juice, presaging the birth of his son, Ganesha. The story can also be connected to the lives of saints, as in this story from Maharashtra state:

> About 300 years ago, a great Saint named Tukaram lived in Maharashtra, India. He was a poor shopkeeper who spent His time chanting and singing devotional songs in the praise of God. His divine behavior alone inspired the people around Him to turn to God and start chanting. However, Saint Tukaram's wife rarely appreciated His greatness and was always angry with Him for not bringing home enough money.
>
> One year, the region was affected by a drought. Many people were starving. One day, Saint Tukaram decided to

harvest the sugarcane from His small farm, to help the situation at home. On His way home with a bullock-cart full of sugarcane, Saint Tukaram saw a poor beggar on the roadside. He was moved by the beggar's plight and gave him some of the sugarcane. This did not stop with the beggar. Due to the severe drought, many people were left starving. On His way home, Tukaram generously gave sugarcane to any starving person He saw. Soon, He had given away all of it except for one stalk.

When Saint Tukaram reached home, His wife was shocked to see this harvest, of a single stalk of sugarcane! Furiously, she questioned Tukaram about it and as usual, He simply and truthfully told her what had happened. She got so furious on hearing what He had done that she violently snatched the sugarcane from Tukaram's hand. As she did, the stalk broke into two pieces.

Saint Tukaram was calm as usual. When the sugarcane stalk broke into two pieces, he smiled and said "God is great. There are now two pieces – one each for the two of us. No one needs to starve!"

Saint Tukaram's wife was taken aback by this response. She immediately felt ashamed for having yelled at her Saintly husband who always faced her anger with loving calmness. Apologising, she fell at the Saint's Feet.[5]

The story illustrates the mystery that generosity begets plenty, while hoarding causes want. The person who hoards fears some future loss and clings to material goods as though nothing good would ever come his or her way again. This consciousness of lack, of privation, leading to a defensive posture about material goods, prevents new opportunities from becoming available, in a negative self-fulfilling prophecy. Lord Ganesha devotion helps to bring about a virtuous cycle in which consciousness of plenty and a purposefully induced state of gratitude lead the devotee to a more open stance towards all forms of wealth. Saint Tukaram's sugarcane led to an attitude of generosity and plenty for all, not only for his neighbors but in his own household as well.

Pomegranates

Pomegranates are said to be a favorite fruit of Lord Ganesha, and they also symbolize the entire universe. They have a rough, leathery exterior which protects the delicate seeds, surrounded by fruit bursting with juices. The pomegranate reminds us of both the bitter and the sweet aspects of life as well as the fact that the surrounding universe provides the sheltering context in which our lives unfold. In some traditions, Ganesha is thought to be the universe itself or to be the ultimate, all-pervading deity. Those who worship him may perceive the infinite blackness of space as suffused with his hidden form.

Clothes, Jewelry

Ganesha and all of the other Hindu gods and goddesses (devas) are treated with respect by dressing them with real clothes and jewelry. Ganesha wears a traditional Indian *dhoti*, a man's garment made of a single woven piece of cloth. Rather like a Western necktie, it can take a good deal of skill to tie the *dhoti* properly, but it looks elegant when donned properly. The accompaniment to the *dhoti* is the *angavastram* scarf, which is artfully draped about the shoulders. In dressing the deity, the householder gives a portion of what he or she has received back to the gods, creating a cycle of blessing. Wealth comes from giving, from keeping the energy moving rather than letting it stagnate. At times, Ganesha will seem like a parent to the devotee, while, at other times, the devotee seems like a parent to this holy child! The sweetness in life comes from the exchange of love, which the *puja* ritual symbolizes in a powerful way.

All jewels come from the earth, a reminder of the plenty of the mother goddess. Gems and jewelry have astrological functions in

Hinduism and are considered a form of medicine. They can also just serve as decoration, and, as royalty, the gods and goddesses deserve the best adornments that the household can afford. A Hindu blessing goes, "May the gods be your wealth," a saying that has many meanings. The household shrine represents and *is* the wealth of the family, both materially and spiritually. On the gross level, the ritual items (puja tray, dishes, bell, censor, etc.) can be quite valuable, and the family builds a storehouse over time. On the subtle and spiritual levels, the devotion shown to God spills over into the devotee's life, developing the true treasures of wisdom, compassion, patience, contentment, and other qualities associated with divinity. The shrine serves as a center for the *shakti*, the divine power, that is the life of the family and the home. Lord Ganesha is the son of Parvati, wife of Shiva, and he holds a special place in Her heart. By placing him in the heart of the home, we also make our home dear to Her, the wellspring of all forms of abundance. By concentrating on Lord Ganesha, all feelings of lack and ill-will depart, as clouds part before the sun.

The Trunk

People don't really have an organ like the elephant's trunk. It has such great dexterity that it can lift up a needle or paint a picture (yes, elephants can and do paint pictures!). On the other hand, it also has the great strength to lift a tree trunk or even knock a tree to the ground. This powerful proboscis can also be used to nuzzle or greet a friend, to guide a baby, take a shower, or eat lunch. Just as people would be at a loss without their hands, elephants would be at a loss without their trunks.

For Lord Ganesha, the trunk represents worldly success and the householder (*grihasta*) path if turned towards his left, and renunciation and the celibate (*sannyasa*) path if turned towards his right. The trunk, when combined with the expression in the eyes, can give an impression of great ferocity and anger, or great kindness and love. Insight comes in viewing these seemingly contradictory aspects as one. In order to truly be kind to ourselves, we must also practice discipline. Severity yields joy. In order to remove the obstacles from our lives, we must allow Ganapati's great strength to flow through us. We want him to turn his more frightful countenance on the demons that beset our lives. These can be recognized as sadness, apathy, anger, greed, and other negative qualities. Just as that mighty elephant trunk can strip a tree branch down to size for easy chewing and digestion, Ganesha can cut problems down to size and make them more easily managed. Dexterity and strength are equally important in the battles of life: it does no good to flail away mindlessly, just as it does no good to impotently gesture in the right direction. The trunk represents what Buddhists call Right Effort, the strength adequate to the task.

IV

Ganesha Mantra

For some years, I have said the Ganesha mantra, *aum gaṃ ganapataye namaḥ,* and have come to understand the mantra on many different levels and in different situational contexts. First, it will be helpful to break down the mantra into its parts and then put it back together again. The first syllable, the holy "aum," cannot be overanalyzed, since it is the seed sound for the entirety of Sanatana Dharma, the eternal natural way, otherwise known as Hinduism. *Aum* is the root mantra of the entirety of creation, the sound from which the worlds came into being and are sustained. It has three sounds, "ah," "ooh," and "mmm," which have a deep and manifold symbolism. These sounds can stand for the three movements of creation, preservation, and destruction, or they can stand for the three primary deities (the Hindu "Trinity") of Brahma (Creator), Vishnu (Preserver), and Shiva (Destroyer). We may associate these deities with the masculine-feminine pairings of Brahma-Saraswati, Vishnu-Lakshmi, and Shiva-Parvati. They can stand for the three gunas, qualities or constituents of nature, which are *rajas* (activity), *tamas* (lethargy), and *sattva* (clarity). The mantra may also stand for the inflowing breath, the retained breath, and the outflowing breath. Many other three-part formulations are possible, and the devotee will come across many of these in her study and meditation. A different sense of this three-fold movement will occur to the devotee at the right time, in accordance with her need and level of realization. "Aum" has come to be associated with the practice of yoga, which, in the West, usually means āsana (postures or poses) practice. It can be quite profound to chant the "aum" in unison with a roomful of people, whether in a yoga studio or temple, and to hear the same sound escaping from your mouth that escapes from the mouths of others, and in turn resonates from the walls. This activity in itself provides a material example of the interconnectedness of all beings, a teaching shared by all of the Indian religions. It is also said, however, that the holy "aum" mantra is the most difficult of all to master, despite, or perhaps because of its simplicity. One could, in principle, recite only the "aum" mantra to complete realization, but this path would be very difficult for most aspirants, who need a little more material for the mind to grasp on its journey.

We come to the next syllable, "*gaṃ*," the seed (bīja) syllable for the god, Ganesha. Each deity has a seed syllable which encapsulates the essence of that aspect of the divine. The "g" here is a hard sound, as in "good." The "a" is soft, closer to a "u," as in "meg*a*byte". The "*ṃ*" sound will sometimes be written as "*ng*," or described as a resonant nasalization. The back of the tongue goes up towards the soft palate," and need not be pronounced with lips pressed together, as in American and British "m" sounds. The sound refers to the deity who is elephant-headed, the remover of obstacles, the refuge of devotees and storehouse of wisdom. An image of Ganesha may be contemplated here, perhaps your favorite piece of devotional art, the image in your home shrine, or something from your own imagination. The important thing here is to invoke the deity to the exclusion of all else. The mantra is normally said in intervals of 108, which equals one rosary or *mala*. It is better to say one rosary with full concentration than to say many rosaries with half-hearted concentration, and the seed sound is effective in this task of training the attention.

The next word in the mantra has two parts, "gana" and "pataye." These words refer to Ganesha's title as "Ganapati," Lord of the Ganas. The Ganas are the attendants or servants of God, and a complex mythology could be described here. For now, it will suffice to think of the *ganas* as akin to the angels in Judeo-Christian tradition, those spirits who carry out the will of God and exist solely for that purpose. Ganesha stands above the rest of the heavenly hosts and can order the spirits as he sees fit. "Pati" means Lord, and the "aye" is necessary for grammatical purposes but also conveys love and respect. The last syllable, *namaA*, is pronounced, "nam-ahah," and it means "we bow to." So the meaning of the whole mantra means, "We convey our respect to the Ruler of the servants of God," or something similar. Any translation will necessarily fall short of the true meaning of the mantra, which can only be revealed through meditation.

Despite the impossibility of the task, we can still attempt to convey a little more clearly what the mantra means, starting with the mundane, everyday sense and then moving to a more inward and spiritual sense. First, it should be said that there is nothing wrong with praying to God for material blessings or for relief from some distressing situation. The mantra is used in this way by millions of devotees around the world, and it remains a valid way to approach Ganesha. If it occupies your mind, it can and should become a topic for prayer. Worries and anxieties can be handed over to God in this way, so that peace can take their place. If you find yourself thinking about a bill that needs to be paid, you cannot advance towards spiritual liberation if your mind is stuck on the bill. Pray for some way to pay the bill, and then your mind will be free for meditation. You cannot force the mind to go where it does not want to go. The mantra, literally, "that which takes away the mind," will gently lead away from preoccupation with mundane things and into contemplation of the divine nature. It will do no good to try to force this to take place: just say the mantra and allow it to take you forward. It is perfectly okay to remain with the worldly sense of the mantra—to pray for money, success, etc.—if that is what has your attention at the time. You may pray in this way for many years before other parts of the mantra begin to open. Just to reiterate one more time, do not pray as you think a "spiritual" person "ought" to pray, but simply be with yourself as you are at that moment. Otherwise you just fool yourself into believing that you have some other nature than the nature that you have, in which case no progress can be made. Just notice whatever thoughts arise and hand them over to the divine nature, to the one who removes obstacles.

Eventually, another sense of the mantra will begin to arise in which you notice that the thoughts themselves are the servants of God and you allow Ganapati to rule your thought process. You will begin to give over the reins of the thought process itself to the Lord. Thoughts may be good or bad, more like the gods (*devas*) or more like the demons (*asuras*). Ultimately, all things, whether good or bad, serve the divine purpose, although this can be difficult to see in the thick of things. The entirety of the universe moves towards union with the divine nature in an unseen drama that unfolds all the time. By saying the mantra, you affirm that you want to consciously enter into this process, that you want to be made aware that all things work together to be brought under the aspect of eternity. You step out of the "driver's seat" of your life and surrender to the divine within, so that your life can become a manifestation of your own divine potential. In this act of the surrender, the ego can be laid bare in its true nature as a fiction, and your divine Self can emerge from hiding. The obstacles, too, will be seen as just bad thoughts, thoughts which the ego creates in order to avoid confronting reality. The mantra works somewhat by subtraction, by taking charge of the thoughts, not aggressively but intentionally, and subverting them to the one goal of achieving peace.

The mantra will finally reach a wordless state where it no longer needs to be repeated either silently or aloud. The energy or *bhava* (devotional feeling) of the mantra takes on a life of its own, and the syllables fall away. It will do no good to return to the repetition at this point because of some arbitrary goal that you may have set for yourself (say three, five, or ten malas). The mantra is the map and not the destination, and once the intuitive sense of the mantra has been gained, the outer sense can fall away. This can be very difficult to achieve with *japa* (recitation) alone, and it is much better and more efficient to pair *japa* with *puja* (ritual worship). *Puja* lays the foundation for *japa,* so that when you go to recite, you have some experiential point of reference that will help you to know the goal which you are pursuing. Some seekers can get confused by great saints like Ramana Maharshi or Ramakrishna, who seemed to do very little ritual worship in the advanced stages of their careers. It must be remembered that they did not begin as pure *jnanis* (devotees who follow the path of knowledge or wisdom) but lived in a cultural context already steeped in worship. One might, theoretically, achieve liberation without *puja* or *japa,* but most people need these material means to get into the proper state of mind. Likewise, silent meditation can be very valuable, but it is also very difficult and is made easier by traditional practices like *puja* and *japa.* The trouble with going straight to silent meditation without any other aid is that it can easily devolve into a daydreaming session or a mental recitation of a to-do list. I have heard of very serious practitioners spending ten or even twenty years at silent meditation while seeing minimal results. These things can be difficult to measure, but feelings of peace, tranquility, love, etc. should accompany the devotion. Otherwise, something is not working properly. If you find yourself with a feeling of stagnation, consult your guru or teacher with the problem. This will be much easier than trying to solve the problem by yourself. Sometimes you may only need a bit of encouragement from someone with more experience.

Another Ganesha Mantra

A bit shorter Ganesha mantra goes, "Aum śrī Ganeshāya namaḥ." We have already said something about the holy syllable "aum." Now we should say something about the term of veneration, śrī, pronounced, "shree." Śrī once held status as a deity in her own right, a goddess associated with the lotus flower and prosperity, much of the territory now covered by the goddess Lakshmī, who presides over all forms of wealth, including natural beauty, material prosperity, and intuitive wisdom. Śrī is not usually worshipped separately today, but her cult (in the sense of formal worship) survives today as a term of respect, which can be applied to gods and holy persons. The name Ganesha means "Lord of Wisdom" or "Chief Disciple," and he has been given the honored position of leading the multitudes into the bliss of realization. He is situated at the gate between worldly and spiritual success, and no one can pass from one to the other without his permission. One may contemplate any image or function of Lord Ganesha while chanting his name and the Lord himself will draw the devotee deeper into worship. You may contemplate his big ears (the better to hear the prayers of devotees), his broken tooth (a blemish that he turned into a tool for writing Mahabharata), or his childlike countenance (for his innocence never fades). Do not worry if you cannot concentrate your mind: this too amounts to one more worry to surrender at the Lord's feet. When you say this mantra, you affirm that you no longer have to go it alone with your meditations, for you now have a powerful ally to guide you along the path. Whatever you might experience in life, Shri Ganesha understands your pain and confusion and will guide you out of it. He has both tenderness and strength, both compassion and might, the qualities that you will cultivate as you sit at his lotus feet.

V

Spiritual Aphorisms

The worship of Ganesha proceeds through several stages. At first, the devotee feels frustration that material aims are not going well but has the good sense and the humility to ask for help. In the next stage, the devotee's aims begin to change to more spiritual ones, such as the desire for renunciation, but the devotee still conceives of the goals and the plans for achieving them. The devotee asks for help, but the basic material for consciousness still derives from the limited self. In the third stage, the devotee gives over the aims to the god and contemplates only what God gives for contemplation. Both the means and the end have been surrendered completely, but a sense of separation remains. In the final stage, all forms of mental rumination have ceased, and the personality and disposition become completely transparent and supple. The personality and the organs of action exist only to reflect the divine radiance, as a prism refracts the light of the sun.

ॐ

Society: drunks in an alley fighting over a handful of change.[6]

ॐ

Be kind to the ego, but don't let it rule you. Let it sit at the table with you, but don't give it all of the food.

ॐ

Now, now, now, now. But gently. Urgency and kindness come

together in the true seeker. Only the person who has both will be able to sustain the spiritual life.[7] Urgency extends to all domains of life: completing mundane tasks, performing spiritual practices (*sadhana*), and most especially, seeking the eternal within the finite. Gentleness should manifest itself in caring for self, caring for other people, and caring for animals and things. Each one of these types of caring is necessary for the others.

ॐ

People create saints to prevent themselves from having to listen to them. Sainthood is the easiest thing of all, the only sane thing. Every other way presents obstacles, every other way leads to insanity.

ॐ

Necessary for sainthood: to stop trying. Only don't call yourself a saint, because the title misleads by creating a cult of personality. All great religious people have taken pains not to distance themselves from others, and yet their followers do exactly that by placing them on pedestals. Trees and rocks are the best saints of all. People create suffering for themselves by imagining that they are different from squirrels, flowers, and streams.[8]

ॐ

We should feel sorry for the ego nature, as if it were a poor lost child wandering alone. It longs for contact with its Parent, the Self or the All.

ॐ

Criticizing the religious beliefs of others, provided those beliefs don't cause any harm, is like saying that water drawn from one well or faucet is inferior to water drawn from another well or faucet. People get thirsty, so they drink. From whatever source it flows, water quenches thirst.

ॐ

You know how to get there: just stop the commentary.

ॐ

Without faith, a *murthi* is just a statue. With faith, it is a window into the world of the gods, a great channel of help in difficult times, a radiant source of healing energy. Making friends with God through puja will make non-believers sneer at you: dharma protects those who follow it by offering this slight form of separation from society.[9] The *devas* appear frightening to the ignorant and sweet to the wise.

ॐ

People keep looking for a New Age according to this or that prophecy. The New Age comes when each one of us takes responsibility for bringing it into our lives. Kindness, patience, love: these qualities inaugurate the New Age. Gardening, meditation, exercise, giving, worship: these practices inaugurate the New Age. Refusing to kill, refusing to hate, refusing to criticize: these abstentions create the New Age. Don't wish for it. Make it happen. Then Ayodhya (the city without war of Ramayana fame) will come on earth and the age of darkness will end.

ॐ

Today you want this, tomorrow you want that. Better to think that what you want today you will not want tomorrow. By thinking in this way, avoid the useless accumulation of things. If this doesn't work, go to a yard sale: see the once-precious possessions on a card table in the rain, sold for a quarter.

ॐ

Sad self, how long will you cling to anxiety? How long will you torture yourself with, "I could have been this, I could have been that." How long will you torture yourself with, "If only I could..." Cast off the anchors of the mind that hold you down. Be at peace now. Live joyfully now. No one else can do it for you.

ॐ

Imagine a clear lake on the horizon. Acres and acres of brambles and thorns stand between you and the clear lake. What should you do to get from here to there? Shred your body to pieces by trampling through the thorns? No. Use circumspect thinking. Look for the hidden path. Make yourself small and the vines and brambles will not hurt you. You will be sitting by that lake soon, serene and unharmed.

ॐ

Who are you? You have been telling yourself stories all this time, casting yourself in plots provided by others. But the best actor is one who does not act. You can only become yourself when you stop striving. This is what is called realizing the Self, which is not identified with any limited concept. Let go and be free.

ॐ

People want money, fame, and success because they think these things will bring peace and contentment. So long as striving remains, there can be no peace and contentment. This is a necessary truth, something that cannot simply be willed to go away. The means must match the end: only peace can lead to peace. Anxiety will never lead to peace: be peaceful now.

ॐ

What can pass through the eye of a needle? Thread, or, better yet, air. Become like the thread or like the air. Only then will the impossible happen.

ॐ

Good influences: Jesus, Buddha, Aristotle, Socrates, Plato, Plotinus, the Stoics. Good influences: Shiva, Krishna, Lakshmi, Sarasvati. Good influences: *The Bible, Tao Te Ching, Bhagavad Gita,* the *Upanishads,* the *Vedas,* the *Dhammapada,* the poems of Rumi. Good influences: Martin Luther King, Jr., Gandhi, Ramana Maharshi, Mother Teresa. Bad influences: shouters, grumblers, complainers. If you must think, keep your thoughts on a high plane.

ॐ

Keep saying *japa* until the mantra manifests itself in feeling. Then let go of the words.

ॐ

Retention of thoughts from the past puts a damper on life transformation. A car can't drive with the parking brake engaged, and a life can't move forward when mired in memory.

ॐ

The temple at Delphi bore the inscription, "Know thyself." But the self that should be known is the Self arriving on the horizon, the person now becoming. This Self, pure and ever-new, sheds the old personality like a snake sheds its skin. Divine, wise, indomitable, it illuminates tired, habitual existence. Hail this Self, the God now arriving! Become this Self that knows no bounds! Become everything! Remember the possibility of the new. Forget the way things have always been. I must evaporate in order for this Self to dawn. And, amazingly enough, it happens. What the sages say does happen: believe this wholeheartedly. Liberation only requires continual belief in the possibility of liberation.

ॐ

At early morning puja, the dipa lamps, with their homemade wicks, won't seem to stay lit. The charcoal for the incense smolders and dies. After much fanning of the flames, worship begins.

ॐ

The voice of temptation is oftentimes not the voice of lust or greed. It's the voice that says, "You're no good. You can't do anything right. You'll never make it. Who do you think you are? You're such a fool." At bottom, this voice really stems from fear, the fear that things will change; the fear of a spirit afraid to die. Let go of this voice, guide it into death, and find freedom. That day will dawn when the nay-saying voice can no longer be heard.

ॐ

Read the scriptures as describing present realities, but if they ever lead you to hatred or pride, burn them.

ॐ

Fire burning bright, never go away!

ॐ

The temple and the home shrine outwardly model inner realities. Serve the deities in the *murthis* so that you can revere them in the *chakras*. Give them your inner real estate, so to speak, by allowing them to shine on the inside of your body. Watch worry and doubt dissolve like clouds before the sun. Truly the *devas* bring forth the best qualities.

ॐ

Lao Tzu says:

> Being and nonbeing give birth to each other,
> Difficult and easy complete each other,
> Long and short form each other,
> High and low fulfill each other,
> Tone and voice harmonize with each other,
> Front and back follow each other—
> it is ever thus.[10]

The wise person knows when to practice maximum exertion and when to relax all effort. Find the flowing region beyond opposites, where effort and passivity meet. All of the opposites have this hidden region of unity. Heraclitus called it the Logos, the union of opposites. This also means that, in the darkness of the spine, there resides a hidden light. In the sad, sinking heart, a hidden joy waits. No one can really understand the Tao or the Way, because it laughs at those who try to tame it. Better to let the Way loose than to try to master it. Keep it in close company, but do not try to put it in a cage. Then the extremes of life become, not manageable, no, but certainly less frightening.

ॐ

Become a sage: other ways lead to suffering and death. The path of wisdom, open to one and all, keeps the hazards of life from becoming mortal wounds. An ounce of philosophy defends against the deepest despair.

ॐ

Shankaraya Shiva! Shankaraya Shiva! The sung words to the *bhajan* resonate through the temple. Hear the blending voices of others as though they were your own voice. Find that point where the voices merge and become one. Hold that point in your ears and in your heart. Feel the actual vibrations of the sound and realize that this is not just an allegory for the divine: God really dwells in the harmonized intentions of sincere devotees. Let yourself slip into the All.

ॐ

The negative emotions of fear, guilt, and hopelessness can serve as indicators for spiritual shams. Beware when any religious teacher attempts to instill them. True religion leads to freedom and joy. False religion leads only to control.

ॐ

Find a place in the woods with a comfortable place to sit. Not too comfortable: a stone, a log, or a patch of pine straw will do. Sit and meditate with eyes closed for thirty minutes or so. Sit and meditate with eyes open for awhile. Observe the naked trunk of a leaning tree, the light shimmering on a stream, the tiny particles that compose the soil. There are many lessons here, waiting to be discovered. After sitting like this for some time, stand and stretch. Then repeat.

ॐ

With training, diligence, and devotion, things reveal themselves as part of an energetic reality, crackling with life. First, remain in the present moment through meditation. Mantra, scripture, and *asanas* can aid in this process as vehicles. The vividness and detail in the world will begin to emerge once the mind has shed distraction. Persist in practice until the attention "muscles" grow stronger. Hold the attentive state with great expectancy. After several hours or over a period of days, the world opens in its true aspect as a divine reality, suffused with radiance.

ॐ

Once I tried to make *modaka* balls from scratch, and I quickly discovered that I didn't have anywhere near the skills of an Indian grandmother. After making the filling from coconut and spices, blending and kneading the dough, and forming the little balls, I thought everything was going pretty well. At this point, I had spent about two hours on my project. The kitchen was wrecked, but I thought I was almost at the finish line. Then I tried frying them in ghee on a stovetop griddle. Instead of being perfect little spheres, they came out like pyramids, because the pan had flattened the sides. So I tried baking them in the oven, and they looked good but were hard as nails. I tried to make sweets but made little cannon balls instead! I offered them to Ganesh at puja the next morning. He said they tasted good, but I think he was just being nice.

ॐ

Call it a rosary or call it a *mala*. It still works the same.

Call it a *mantra* or a prayer. It works the same.

Call it a hymn or a *bhajan*. Both work the same.

The value lies not in the outward form but in the hidden essence. You have heard all of this before, no doubt. Become light and supple, then. Stop thinking and start doing.

ॐ

The traffic light is red. Aum.
The traffic light is green. Aum.
I'm late for my appointment. Aum.
Aum, aum, aum.

ॐ

Did you think that you would go on waiting forever? Did you think this path went nowhere? Look how despair slipped into your house, under the door, and straight into your nostrils. You gave it a millimeter, a centimeter, an inch, and it took your body, your house, your clothes, your cutlery. Despair sat down to breakfast with your wife and drove your car, did your job. Evict despair. The time has come for that old wish to become reality. It's here! Answer the door.

ॐ

Stop looking for a power outside. Look within.

ॐ

Not one single thing in the universe lies outside of the divine.

Therefore, don't worry about the supposed dangers of idolatry. Remember the divinity of everything and nothing will go wrong.

ॐ

Oh, sweet cow! They called you a slab of meat, carved you into bits and pieces, said you had no thoughts or feelings. Look how good you are! Your eyes are so gentle. The tuft of hair on top of your head reminds me of a child after awaking from sleep. You chew and rest, enjoying the company of the herd. You never kill or cheat. You never ask for more than your fair share. Little wonder that Shiva and Krishna keep company with you. If only everyone could see your beauty, innocence, and wisdom!

ॐ

Do you not see the cloud of *asuras* (demons) swirling about your head? Anger, jealousy, sadness, worry: these are the real demons that take the joy out of life. Conquer them with love and peace. Choose love and peace. Keep fighting for love and peace. The *devas* (gods) will help, but don't think that they will do all the work.

ॐ

Everyone keeps talking about the supposed decline in family life and the dangers of the loss of traditional values. You can't create strong families by shouting and legislation. Love makes a family. Love is the only tradition worth preserving, no matter who does the loving. Don't let preachers and politicians use the family as an excuse for accruing power for themselves. If more people would recognize this bid for power, this insatiable craving for influence, for the sham that it is, it would go away. If they really cared about children and families, they would provide good food, education, and medical care. That might actually make a difference. Fear-mongering only generates fear.

ॐ

Peace, *shanti*, ends prayers, along with *aum*, the primal sound, because the universe, at its heart, radiates eternal peace. The great *rishis* teach that the axis mundi, the center of the world, is also the axis of each person's spine. "Microcosm is macrocosm" goes the alchemical dictum common to many traditions of esotericism. This may seem egocentric—to think that the spine is the center of the world and even of the universe—but egotism actually arises from a lack of this calm center. The craving mind arises when we think that something "out there" can bring peace. Begin. Becoming aware of peace is the "one thing needful." With practice, you can become aware within a few minutes of meditating. Begin and begin again. With even more practice, you can become aware while doing anything. With even more practice, you no longer need practice because the whole of life has become practice. Pause many times each day, at the end of every activity, to say, "Aum, shanti, shanti, shanti. Aum, peace, peace, peace." Do not just think this, as a wish, but realize that it is so.

ॐ

Each person sees the world through a filter or cloud of pre-occupations, plans, and projects, conceiving and categorizing every event, person, and thing, as useful or not useful, desirable or repulsive. This mental process prevents seeing the world in its true nature. The stream of thoughts must be slowed. Silences must be inserted into this incessant inner monologue. Then the observing mind must step back from this dialogue and watch it. Gradually the categorizing, judging mind begins to relax and weaken. It will never go away, and, indeed it has its uses, but it will begin to soften and change its nature. Why does this process work? It works because the thought process has disentangled from the ego. The horses have come un-reined, so to speak, and so they can graze peacefully. It takes a good deal of trust in order to let this happen. We must, first of all, believe that the world will continue to support us even in the absence of fierce competition. We must also believe in the divinity of other souls, other lives, and that the same mystery is hidden in "them" that is hidden in ourselves.

ॐ

Congratulations, you have arrived! This is the moment for which you were born. Are you ready to live it? To stop worrying all of the time? To put every last plan into motion? Look how the sun has risen in the sky another day! Look how you have been crowned with another moment of infinite goodness! Look out the window and see the body of God! Each leaf, each speck of dirt glows with radiance. The hour for sadness has long past. Awake, awake, awake! No more gloom! No more gloom! Only joy.

Did you know that you have been chosen to behold God? Did you know that you belong to the mind of God? Did you know that you are divine, that you are God? Why do you quake with fear? Why do you always assume the worst will happen? Why do you color experience with such dreary tones? Dance and shout for joy! Everything will be fine and more than fine! Claim your own joy and bring joy to the world! Nothing can hurt you anymore!

ॐ

People live at the mercy of their thoughts most of the time. "I am cranky," "I am angry," "I am sad": these states seem like the weather, uncontrollable. In fact, a very subtle path exists which can make such unpleasant feelings more manageable. First, realize that thoughts and emotional shadings interact with each other: a positive internal dialogue will lead to positive emotional states and vice versa. Second, become aware of awareness. This seems silly, tautological even, but most people have no idea that they create their own experiences. Observe the thoughts and feelings as they arise, and then practice governing them. This does not have to be an aggressive activity. A very small rudder can steer a massive ship. So the small internal adjustments make a big change in direction. We don't just have emotions: we emote. "Thinking positively" has its place, but the negative emotions and thoughts have a role to play as well. Most of the time, the negative emotions and thoughts just cause high blood pressure and premature aging, but they need not simply be causes of stress. The negative emotions can be cues for action. Maybe anger can lead to better communication with a partner. Maybe frustration can lead to a new business venture. If allowed to fester, negative emotions can eat away at our minds and bodies. When given positive outlets, negative emotions can act as catalysts for change. Giving the negative emotions vectors for expression will deflate them and transform them.

ॐ

Work, in the world or in the home, should not be denigrated as inherently unspiritual. If pursued with patience and care, it can become an occasion for unleashing the *shakti* power, the emanations of the divine. The gods help those who help themselves, yes, but this phrasing would be too simplistic for the kind of care that they have for humankind. What would be the point of success if it comes at the expense of peace and fulfillment? What does it mean to "get things done" if this doing has no loving qualities? Rather, endeavor to bring God and the gods along in every activity, every doing. Keep their images in sight at all times. Make your environment hospitable for practice. Play a *bhajan* on the stereo or the internet and let the work flow, with the help of the *devas*. As you praise them, your own work will be crowned with glory, a glory that other people cannot help but notice.

ॐ

What is work but a series of activities, a series of events? It takes effort even to stay in bed, to pour a glass of soda, to go talk with friends. Everything requires effort, even sitting still. This means that work is not a special domain of its own; however it might appear on the outside. Spiritually-minded people often shy away from working too hard, fearing crude materialism. We should, indeed, work with a still mind and a loving heart, but we should also work steadily and dynamically. "Personal" and "professional" should blend together, as the warp and weft of life. Emphasize one too much and the whole thing comes apart.

ॐ

To learn about work, watch someone making something by hand—a potter or a woodcarver, a painter. Look at the care that goes into the piece, the precision of a curve, the steady hand and eye. Work like this and find total confidence. Take the pride of an artist in a spreadsheet or presentation. It may seem silly, but this attitude makes all the difference.

ॐ

The elements aid in the completion of work. Whenever possible, sit near a window, and, if possible, open the window. Enjoy the sounds of birds and the feel of the breeze. Even in harsher climates, a brief trip outside restores the mind and senses. Millions today work in sterile environments, never seeing natural light or taking a step outside. The design of buildings and office parks leave much to be desired in the way of mature trees and openness to the outside. Most landscaping amounts to little more than a strip of grass and some scrawny shrubs, far less than needed for a human habitation. Make the most of a drab environment by taking a quick walk. Keep plants nearby. Sneak a flower or leaf into a drab cubicle. By all means, compensate for time spent in such environments by spending more time outside in off hours. Even going to the gym does not have all of the benefits of outdoor activity. Realize that people need plants and animals in order to thrive, and that these other creatures feed human creativity. Productivity without creativity may "get the job done," but if the work does not have transformative potential, it will wither and die when conditions change.

ॐ

Snow, wind, rain, hail—these forces that most people find mildly annoying have messages to speak. They tell us that we, too, Lords of Nature that we pretend to be, have vulnerabilities. They teach us about the sensitivity of our skin, our need for protection and warmth. They tell us that we, too, are mortal. And they can be company in solitude. Who has not listened in rapt attention to the plinking of rain on a roof? The pattern goes beyond randomness: it is the sound of the universe itself, a message from the depths of all being. The person who can read the rain will never be alone, will always have a refuge in difficult times. The rain can be the best companion: it understands our sorrows, speaks our grief into the puddles that gather on sidewalks. Of course, it can also be joyful and playful, play jokes and laugh. To most "adults," this talk can only be classified as nonsense, romantic babble or mystical obfuscation. But these are the lessons our culture must learn or re-learn in order to find some kind of peace or health. In all seriousness, failure to listen, failure to pay attention, leads to sickness and death. Because we learn to turn away from natural sources of satisfaction, we seek extra stimuli to make up the difference and eventually over-consume. This over-consumption causes all kinds of diseases that could have been prevented by simply going for a walk or listening to the wind in the trees.

ॐ

Children understand the elements better than most adults. My son and his cousin once spent half an hour stomping in the puddles in a restaurant parking lot while the adults dealt with a mix-up in the reservations. For children, icicles become scepters or swords: a field of snow can provide *days* of entertainment. Only the weather report resolves the sensory world into facts and numbers, making a world of play into the choice of whether or not to wear a sweater. We should greet the morning as a friend, but we greet it as an adversary to be conquered. Those of us who have forgotten how to play must re-claim that ability, and thereby become children.

ॐ

Maturity, wisdom, is nothing other than the ability to find work in play and play in work.

ॐ

Perhaps you hope for a magic formula that will make life a little easier. Find lightness and buoyancy. Move nimbly from task to task and solve problems without dwelling on them. Be light and quick. Yoga teaches that the *tamasic,* heavy qualities (like lethargy, depression, etc.) impede development. In order to counter them, use activity (*rajas*) but never let that activity become too aggressive. Balance it with clarity and light (*sattva*). A proper balance of forces is the most potent magic.To learn about *sattva*, look at a tree in wintertime, without any leaves. Nothing blocks the sun from hitting its trunk. It has nothing to hide.

ॐ

To become whole, to heal the wounds of the past and no longer fear the future, make this present dynamic. Pour every ounce of energy into this present. Work and realize. Realize and work. No effort ever goes wasted, because it all goes back into the play at the heart of existence. Learn from rejection, sadness, disappointment, and failure. Make them into your tools and teachers. Don't dwell on the past, but do unravel its secrets. Unlock yourself and solve the riddle you present to yourself. Untie the knots that bind. Awake to a new reality, one undetermined by the past. Live a new future, a new dream. Allow its spell to fall over you. Listen to it whispering. Imagine what it would be like to no longer be ignored, to be respected and heard. Imagine what it would be like to have plenty, not to hoard but to have plenty, and imagine giving to others. Allow that imagining to expand, fill consciousness and become real in the world.

ॐ

Can you become rich just by thinking about it? The question has been posed in the wrong way. By fixating on a narrow definition of wealth, namely a number in a bank account or stock portfolio, popular culture misses wealth altogether. Wealth can also be measured in the health of communities, in parks and libraries, in the minds of children. The notion of private property actually makes for less wealth, because it separates people from one and other and makes them think of 'me' and 'mine.' Everyone owns the landscape, the streets, the houses, even without socialism or anarchism. Stop thinking you have to hold the deed to things. You own them without owning them. Yogaswami of Sri Lanka said, "Did you know that I have all the money in all the banks of the world?" Understand his meaning and be rich.

ॐ

Does this mean that working for money is bad? On the contrary, earning money is one of the aims of life. Earn as much of it as you can without losing integrity. Only do not confuse integrity with simply acting within the bounds of the law or being "successful" in a career. That integrity ultimately comes down to a hidden destiny tied to each individual person. Sanatana Dharma teaches that the real goal is liberation from rebirth, but the ways of getting there are different for each soul. The path can only be revealed through practice, through the counsel of a preceptor, through retreats and pilgrimages, and through the help of the *devas*. We all must sometimes walk "blind," without knowing if the action is correct, but signposts along the way help tremendously. Only don't denigrate the body: it is the vehicle through this journey.

ॐ

Recognize the fleeting as fleeting, the enduring as enduring. Peace owes its origin to this discernment.

ॐ

You complain of a hectic life, of the way the world never grants a moment's rest. Remember that you, too, belong to the world, and that you steer its course. An axe splits hard wood by its sharp edge, weight, and design. With the right technique, very little force is needed. Use the sharp edge, the weak points in the wood. Strike in the right manner, hitting the right places, and you will not grow tired before the end of the job.

ॐ

Will the situation be better a year from now? Will things ever get any easier? Work today, practice today, and craft a better tomorrow.

ॐ

Ask each morning for three assignments: one way to make someone else happy, one way to solve nagging problems, and one way to draw closer to the divine.

ॐ

Holy books crowd library shelves and bookstores. Never before have so many esoteric secrets, so many of the world's religions, been laid bare before so many. Throw a rock and hit a guru in the head, open any publication and find a spiritual teacher. So much advice: some of it bad, some of it good. Some crooked teachers, some wise and kind.

Imagine a game of roulette with high stakes: nothing less than the future is on the line. This is the game that people play with religion. Some choose to play it safe and stay out of the game altogether. Others risk little and gain little. Some lose everything, and some gain everything.

A businessman came and stood before a roulette wheel. A stranger came and whispered a number in his ear. He played the number and won. Each time the wheel spun, the stranger gave him a new number. Each time the little ball landed in the spot that the stranger indicated. Each time the man doubled or quadrupled his money. This happened three more times, and the businessman began to feel invincible. The stranger whispered a fourth number in the man's ear, and he put everything on that number. The little ball bounced to a completely different number, and the businessman lost all of his earnings.

"Why did you tell me the wrong number?" the businessman said to the stranger. "Did you want me to lose everything?"

"Look," said the stranger. "I gave you knowledge of the impossible, made you know what you could not have known. You put down the money: you made the choices. I get one number wrong and you complain that it's not fair?"

So it is with religion: sometimes it's good to heed the advice of strangers, but remember that the choices belong with each person. Religious experience reveals things that should not be known by mere mortals, and yet it also carries heavy risks.

ॐ

Regard everything as holy.

ॐ

We live our lives within material reality, as things among things, and yet this materiality can be transcended for those with "eyes to see" and "ears to hear."[11]

What for the devoted
Does not serve as an instrument
To attain identification with you?
And what, then, for the spiritually inferior,
Does not serve as an obstacle,
Leading to failure in spiritual attainment?[12]

A certain kind of seeing leads to liberation. This kind of seeing knows everything as suffused with a hidden, divine reality. At first this must be taken on faith, but, with intense devotion, intense searching, it blossoms into sight. The senses themselves do not mislead: they simply do not have the whole story. Or rather, the senses must be trained not to flit this way and that: they must be taught to remain in one place, to see through or see into this present reality. One may set aside some pleasures in order to achieve this, but the reward comes in the form of a transformed mundane reality, so that the most simple things positively glow with radiance. Very few people have seen this, because very few put themselves through the discipline required to see it. Having a spiritual life requires time and effort: teachers who promise instant results, more likely than not, just want to make a quick buck. Surprising, wonderful things do happen, but usually as a result of sincere seeking.

ॐ

Children cannot wait to leave school on the last day before summer. They burst out the doors, into the yard, onto buses and sidewalks. Such should be the feeling of a devotee on a day of retreat, on going out to join the dance of Shiva.

ॐ

Prefer forests, monasteries, ashrams, and temples for days of *sadhana*, and yet realize that any place will do. Set aside places and times. Hide away hours like change in a piggy bank. The day will come to break it open.

ॐ

The person who sees the finitude of life will not squander time. Every intention and action will be focused on living a full life. Those rescued from the jaws of death teach the lesson of savoring every moment, making each day, each minute count.

ॐ

Each person contributes something to society and makes the whole thing go—even the drifters and runaways. The whole future of the world could depend on a single human being, and no one knows who that person might be. For that matter, the future might also depend on a single frog or an earthworm. It's all interconnected. Darwin called it the tangled bank: each species depends on all the others. Best to tread lightly and value everything and everyone. Interdependence isn't just some floaty notion: it's the way the world works.

ॐ

A flame burns so steadily and brightly, until all of the fuel has been exhausted. Capture that steadiness.

ॐ

Every spring the earth awakes. New blades of grass spring from brown turf, the robins peck the soil, the squirrels resume their chatter. Everything has its cycles. The day, too, emerges from dawn to noonday to dusk to darkness. People too have their seasons and times, and all this is quite normal. It is only when dormancy lasts for years that it indicates a problem. States of torpor will come every now and again, but somnolence should not be a way of life. Every life should have an element of dynamism, a noonday sun, and an element of rest, the moon. When the cycles get interrupted, trouble begins. Disorder can be repaired by restoring natural rhythms, ups and downs.

ॐ

The emotions crest and fall like waves: they do not determine the meaning of an event or the value of that event. Suffering can be reduced by uncoupling the emotion from the associated event. This approach, the one taught by the Stoics, the Buddha, and various schools of yoga, does not amount to repression. The method of detachment does not try to forcefully deal with the emotions at all: it simply steps back from them and observes them. This observation produces insights into the nature of the emotions. Like wild creatures, they have their own intensities and directions. See them as part of the mental landscape, neither bad nor good. Do not try to tailor events to the dictates of the emotions, because it will be futile.

ॐ

When trouble comes, retreat into meditation. Gaze out on the body and realize it to be a thing of the world, that is, material. See the way the light and air play across the skin in just the same way that they play across the furniture, the windowsill, the lamp, the wall. See how the elements that compose the world also make the organs, teeth, and hair. See how thoughts, too, arise from the world and return to the world. See how everything circulates, and let sorrow circulate as well. Let it go out into the world: don't hold onto it.

ॐ

Throw down your arms: enough of fighting! Mental entanglements can be just as violent as a boxing match and just as tiring. Let them go. "But they keep coming back," you say. Let them go again. And so on. Rinse and repeat.

ॐ

Van Gogh's "Starry Night" or his "Café Terrace at Night" do not "represent" the world, if by that is meant some kind of literal copy. However, these paintings do represent the world more accurately than a photograph in capturing the vitality of things and situations, the way that lights can dance past our eye sockets and into our hearts. Both artists and mystics know how to orient themselves towards things and landscapes: they know how to tap into the depths of surfaces. They intentionally take pleasure in things most people would not notice.

ॐ

You may ask yourself: do I really need to say mantras on a *rudraksha* mala or *tulsi* beads? Can't I just count on my fingers or in my head? Do I really need to wear a *dhoti* or *kurta* for my morning *sadhana*? Won't sweatpants do just as well? Do I really need a *murthi* of my chosen divinity? Can't I just form a picture in my head? Those of us from Western societies, especially, sometimes shy away from Indian traditions that we regard as "cultural." We may sometimes feel awkward learning new ways of doing things, even though these ways are actually quite old on a global scale. Go ahead and feel awkward: only know that wisdom resides in the formalities, so they can't be dismissed out of hand. Doing *puja* and *japa* in the traditional way will advance practice much faster than mental discipline alone. The religious items themselves are like externalized meditations: that's why it's so important to stick to traditions of yoga. Ritualized worship actually makes the inner visualizations much easier and more potent. This is why it is so important to worship in the temple and have times set aside for *sadhana*. Yes, you can pray to the deities while driving a car, but without that anchor of formal practice, the informal practice will not be effective. This isn't just a matter of dogmatism or traditionalism: we do these things because they work. Doing them half-heartedly or not doing them at all will produce meager results.

Fulfillment begins when complaining ceases. This should not be taken in a "shut up and take your medicine" sort of way. Complaints should not be suppressed: this will never get rid of them. It will merely push them into the subconscious where they will take much longer to resolve. A better way of dealing with negativity begins with deliberate enjoyment. In this world which Hindus call the Kali Yuga, the Iron Age, ugliness and discord abound. So it becomes that much more important to notice and cherish beauty and concord when they arise. Notice and cherish: this practice produces a more contented frame of mind, but it isn't always easy. "Stop and smell the roses" goes the cliché, but this phrase is a little too passive. The roses may well be on a different path, or they may need to be planted first. Or maybe the path is crowded and people are pushing and shoving. Making peace means finding calm within, and with this inner calm comes a more ready frame of mind in which one can actually enjoy the world.

ॐ

The hellish planes of existence should be seen as torturous mental states available to us on this earth. One of the pre-eminent hells of our time lies in thinking of everything in terms of its exchange value or cash value. By this means, all people become cogs in one great machine. Once the standard of exchange value has been adopted, a corporate executive is actually worth many hundreds of times more than a day laborer. This preposterous fiction must be abandoned, for it has horrendous moral effects. Our *sadhana* must teach the innate divinity residing within all things and all people, all subject to change and dissolution but all equally holy. By this means alone can we avoid the hellish state of mind that insists on cash value alone. We prostrate ourselves before Nandi, the bull mount of Lord Shiva and a symbol of constancy, and not before the bull of Wall Street, the deification of greed. Markets have no caring or kind capacities, and we must compel them by our own efforts to operate according to spiritual principles. Think of the city of Lanka in the Rāmāyāna: the demons have the most splendid palaces, the most sumptuous food and drink—even beautiful temples with priests chanting mantras. Wealth can be bent to good or evil purposes, so we must avoid looking on the outward show of wealth as a sign of divine blessing.

Appendix: Ganesha Puja

How to Perform Home Puja

Home puja can be a wonderful way to invite the deities and the qualities they represent into your life. The text given below is remarkably compact and takes about half an hour after the devotee has gained some proficiency. It is quite normal to feel awkward at first. Chanting in Sanskrit while completing the ritual actions can be difficult. You may wish to recite the text and read the instructions a few times while making notes to yourself before doing the actual ritual. Then you will need some basic supplies, which are listed below. The elements of worship can range from costly statues and implements that cost thousands of dollars to simple handmade clay containers and images. You will have to determine what fits into your budget and where the items will be situated in your place of residence. A complete science called Vaastu is devoted towards arranging the home and altar properly, but, to begin, you can just choose a spot that is as quiet and out of the way as possible. It is customary to place the altar low to the ground so that the devotees can sit before the deity, but families with small children may place the image on a mantel or other high place (open flames being somewhat dangerous for little hands). A separate room for a home temple would be most ideal, but that may not be realistic for your household. Do not overlook outdoor locations, as long as the deity can be reasonably sheltered from the sun, wind, and rain.

Indian stores will sell puja items, and they can be found online easily. Make the puja as luxurious as you are able for the deity, but do not overextend yourself financially by buying items you cannot afford. It is perfectly acceptable to substitute items where necessary or to omit part of the puja if you do not have the appropriate item. My own guru offered leaves when he was living as a wandering *sadhu* in India and could not afford the more expensive worship elements. You may wish to purchase your puja vessels and deity sets one at a time, so that the process does not become overwhelming. If you are good at crafts, you can make your own deity clothes to the size of your image.

Supplies Needed:
Deity statue (*murthi*) or coin
Seat or shrine for the deity
Clothes and adornments for the deity
Fresh fruit, food, and flowers
Raw, unbroken rice grains (may be dyed yellow with turmeric)
Incense
Water (Ganges water ideal)
Water pot or cup
Water pitcher
Food plate
Incense stand or tray
Bell
Lamp and wicks or candle
Oil or clarified butter (*ghee*)
Holy ash (*vibhuti* or *bhasma*)
Sandal paste (*chandana*)
Red powder (*kum kum*)

Once you have acquired the necessary items and practiced your mantras a few times, you are ready to begin! Remember that the puja ritual is a guided meditation designed to take the work out of meditation. Simply by performing the actions and saying the mantras with care, you will automatically be brought into a meditative state.

Complete Text and Instructions

Reprinted with Permission of Himalayan Academy, Kauai, Hawaii, originally appearing in *What is Hinduism?*, chapter 24.

I. Āchamanam Water Sipping by the Pūjāri

Aum sumukhāya svāhā
Aum ekadantāya svāhā
Aum gajakarṇakāya svāhā

Aum! Hail to the God whose face is always shining!
Aum! Hail to the God who has only one tusk!
Aum! Hail to the God with huge elephant ears!

Holding the spoon with your left hand, take a spoonful of water from the cup and place it in the right palm to rinse the hand, letting the excess fall onto the floor or a tray. Put another spoonful of water into the right hand, intone "Aum sumukhāya svāhā" and sip the water. Repeat for the second and third lines, then rinse the right hand again.

II. Vighneśvara Prārthanā Ganeśa Invocation

Aum śuklāmbaradharam vishṇum
śaśivarṇaṁ chaturbhujam
prasanna vadanaṁ dhyāyet
sarvavighnopaśāntaye

Aum. O Lord dressed in splendid white, pervading the universe, shining radiantly like rays of the full moon, having four mighty arms and a charming, happy face, we meditate on you that all obstacles may be quelled.

Salute Lord Gaṇeśa by holding hands in añjali mudrā, the prayerful pose. Then, while reciting the verse, tap your temples lightly with your knuckles three times. Alternatively, you may cross your arms before your face, the left hand tapping the right temple and vice versa. Return your hands to añjali mudrā while reciting the last words of the chant.

III. Saṅkalpa Statement of Purpose

[**ushaḥ kāla**, dawn
prātaḥ kāla, morning
madhyāhnakāla, noon
sāyaṅkāla, evening
ūrdhvayāmakāla, night]

Aum adya pūrvokta evaṅguṇasakala
viśesheṇa viśishṭāyām asyāṁ śubhatithau
Aum Mahāgaṇeśvaraṁ uddiśya
Mahāgaṇeśvara prītyartham
Mahāgaṇeśvara prasāda siddhyartham
yathā śakti (chant name of city) **deśe** (insert the time of day, above)
dhyānāvāhanādi Gaṇeśa pūjāṁ karishye
Aum apa upaspṛiśya

At this particularly auspicious moment, time and place, on this auspicious day, so that we may realize the fullness of your grace, to the best of our ability this (insert time of day) Gaṇeśa pūjā we shall now perform. Aum. By touching pure water we become pure.

While reciting this statement of purpose, take a pinch of rice and hold it at chest height in your closed right palm, with open left hand underneath. Insert the time of day and the place where indicated. As you chant the last word, karishye, gently toss the rice toward the base of the image. Then, with the left hand, place a spoonful of water into your right palm and ritually wash both hands with the water by wiping the palms together a few times as you recite "Aum apa upa spṛiśya." Once the saṅkalpam has been chanted, the pūjā must not be interrupted or abandoned until the concluding mantras are recited.

IV. Āvāhanam, Āsanam Welcoming and Offering a Seat

dhyāyāmi, āvāhayāmi, ratnasiṁhāsanaṁ samarpayāmi

We now meditate on you, O Lord, and invite you to sit upon the jewel-studded, lion throne we have prepared for you.

Offer a pinch of rice to the Deity as you chant each of the three words before "samarpayāmi." Visualize Gaṇeśa seated on a gem-studded throne before you, smiling, full of blessings, waiting to be honored as a guest in your home.

V. Arghyam Washing the Lord's Feet and Hands

pādayoḥ pādyam samarpayāmi
hastayoḥ arghyam samarpayāmi

We now humbly bathe each of your white lotus feet and gently wash each of your precious hands, Lord Gaṇeśa.

With your right hand offer a spoonful of pure water by holding it up before the Deity momentarily and then placing it in the tīrtha cup. This is how all water offering is done throughout the pūjā. As you chant the first line, visualize yourself bathing the feet of Gaṇeśa. Offer a second spoonful of pure water as you intone the next line and visualize yourself washing His hands.

VI. Āchamanam Offering Water to Quench His Thirst

Aum bhūr-bhuvaḥ suvaḥ āchamanīyaṁ samarpayāmi

Aum! In all three worlds, we humbly offer you fresh, pure water for sipping.

VII. Snānam Ritual Bathing

Aum surasindhu samānītam suvarṇakalaśāsthitam
snānārthaṁ gṛihyatām śambho salilam vimalam gaṇeśa
gaṅgāsnānam samarpayāmi

We now bathe you, beloved Lord Gaṇeśa, the pure one, with the water that was brought from the Ganges in the golden pot. We have bathed you in sacred Gaṅgā water.

While ringing the bell and reciting this verse, dip a flower into the tīrtha water and gently sprinkle the Deity. Do this three times or more. Hold the flower in your right hand in the mṛigi mudrā, the stem between your third and fourth fingers. If the altar design allows, you may pour water over the mūrti, rather than sprinkling it during this chant.

VIII. Alaṅkāram Adornment and Offerings

vastrārtham maṅgalākshatān samarpayāmi
upavītārtham maṅgalākshatān samarpayāmi
Aum gandhaṁ gṛihāṇa surabhim andhakā surasūdana,
kuṅkumadi samāyuktaṁ kulāchalaniketana
divya parimala vibhūti chandana
kuṅkumam samarpayāmi

We give you this auspicious unbroken rice, our magnificent Lord, that you may enjoy resplendent clothing. We give you auspicious unbroken rice, Lord Gaṇeśa, that you may be handsomely adorned with a white, cotton sacred thread. Aum. O Lord, the destroyer of the demon Andhakāsura, you who resides in the Himālayas, please accept the good smelling *chandana* with *kuṅkuma* and choice offerings.

Dress the Deity. Offer a pinch of unbroken rice while chanting each of the first two lines. Repeat the third and fourth lines over and over as you decorate the Deity with flowers. The last line is recited once while applying vibhūti (holy ash), chandana (sandalpaste) and kuṅkuma. (red powder).

IX. Pushpam Offering Flowers

tadupari maṅgalākshatān samarpayāmi pūjārtham
nānāvidhapatra pushpāṇi samarpayāmi

We now offer this auspicious unbroken rice. And for the fulfillment of our devotion, we offer many kinds of fresh, blooming flowers, our peerless Lord.

A pinch of rice is offered with the first line. A handful of flowers is offered with the second.

X. Dhūpam Offering Incense

Aum vanaspatyudbhavaiḥ divyaiḥ
nānāgandhasamanvitaiḥ,
āghreyadhūpadīpānām dhūpo-yam pratigṛihyatām.
daśāṅgam guggulopetam sugandhan sumanoharam,
āghreyaḥ sarvadevānām dhūpo-yam pratigṛihyatām.
dhūpamāghrāpayāmi
dhūpānantaram āchamanīyam samarpayāmi
maṅgalākshatān samarpayāmi

The finest incense, of magical qualities, of full and varied fragrances, Lord Gaṇeśa, we set aflame and offer to you in this, our home. Incense of the finest resins and perfumes, incomparable in sweetness and aroma, to be inhaled and enjoyed by you and all the Gods and devas, we offer to you in this, our home. Eagerly we offer to you, our resplendent Lord, fine resin incense, of heavenly odor, bewitching to the mind, rising out of a ghee-fed flame. We offer it to you in this, our home. This fine incense we have duly offered for your pleasure. And we again offer you cool, sweet water for sipping and auspicious unbroken rice.

During this chant, make three circles before the Deity with lighted incense held in your right hand while ringing the bell with your left hand. Complete the third circle and trace an Aum as you chant the fifth line, dhūpamāghrāpayāmi. At that point raise the incense higher and ring the bell louder. Put the incense down, and recite the next two lines. With the first, water is offered, with the second, a pinch of rice.

XI. Dīpam Offering the Light

aum sājyavarti trayopetam prājyamaṅgala dāyakam,
dīpam paśya dayārāśe dīnabandho namo-stu te.
aum āvāhitabhyaḥ sarvabhyo devatabhyo namaḥ,
divya maṅgala dīpaṁ sandarśayāmi,
dīpānantaramāchamanīyaṁ samarpayāmi,
maṅgalākshatān samarpayāmi

O the Compassionate, the friend of devotees! See this lamp offered which is lighted with ghee and three wicks and which is the provider of abundant auspiciousness.

Salutations to you!

Aum! Salutations to all the Gods invoked! This divine, auspicious light we offer to you. After that, we offer you pure water for sipping and auspicious unbroken rice.

Offer the oil light to Lord Gaṇeśa and ring the bell as you chant this hymn. As with the incense, circle three times then draw the Aum with the flame. Then raise the flame and ring the bell louder, then stop ringing. Offer water, then a flower or a pinch of rice.

XII. Naivedyam Offering Food

satyaṁ tvartena *(chant if in morning)*
ṛitaṁ tvā satyena *(if evening)* **parishiñchāmi**
Aum amṛitamastu amṛitopastaraṇamasi svāhā
Aum gaṇeśāya svāhāhā, Aum gaṇeśāya svāhāhā,
Aum gaṇeśāya svāhāhā

We add Truth to Truth. Aum. May this sweet and pungent food be transformed into nectar. We humbly offer to you this food.

While reciting the first part of the mantra, uncover the food offering. Then, while chanting the last line and ringing the bell, circle a spoonful of water over the food and offer it to the Deity. While ringing the bell softly, gently waft the aroma and vital essences of the food or fruit towards the Deity. Do this by sweeping the right hand over the food with a flower held between your fingers, stem upward. The palm is facing downward as it moves over the food, then rotates upward as the sweep approaches the Deity, bringing the aroma and prāṇa toward His nose and mouth. As you complete the third line, gently toss the flower toward the feet of the Deity at the end of the sweep with all the love in your heart.

Aum āvāhitābhyaḥ sarvābhyo devatābhyo namaḥ,
nānā vidha mahānaivedyaṁ nivedayāmi,
yathāśakti samarpita mahānaivedyam kṛipayā svīkuru

Aum! Salutations to all the Gods invoked! Because we are offering you our very best, Lord Gaṇeśa, in all sincerity and love, please consider the essence of this food as among the finest meals you have ever received. To the best of our ability in the worship of you, we offer this food and humbly beg that you will receive it.

Ringing the bell loudly as you recite the above chant, pick up a flower or a pinch of rice and hold it at chest height in the fingertips of the right hand. As the last word is spoken, gently release the rice or flower at the feet of the Deity. Then put down the bell and raise your hands above your head in devout prayer that Gaṇeśa will accept the meal. While your hands are raised, close your eyes and visualize Gaṇeśa accepting and partaking of the meal. After a moment, lower your hands and intone Aum quietly.

XIII. Vighneśvarāshṭottara Śatanāmāvaliḥ Chanting Gaṇeśa's 108 Names

In this section of the pūjā, chant the "garland of Gaṇeśa's 108 *names." As you intone each name, offer with your right hand a flower, some flower petals or a pinch of rice. The names are attributes of the Deity, each delineating an aspect of His wondrous nature. Each name is preceded by the mantra Aum and followed by namaḥ, meaning "obeisance, adoration or homage to." Thus the first line is chanted Aum Vināyakāya Namaḥ (pronounced, "na-ma-ha").*

Vināyakāya *...the remover (of obstacles)*
Vighnarājāya *...the ruler of obstacles*
Gaurīputrāya *...the son of Gaurī*
Gaṇeśvarāya *...the lord of categories*
Skandāgrajāya *...Skanda's elder brother*
Avyayāya *...the inexhaustible one*
Pūtāya *...the pure one*
Dakshāya *....the dexterous one*
Adhyakshāya *...the great presider*
Dvijapriyāya *...who loves the twice-born*
Agnigarvacçhide *...who destroyed fire's ego*
Indraśrīpradāya *...who restored Indra's wealth*
Vāṇīpradāya *...who gives eloquence*
Avyayāya *...the inexhaustible one*

***Sarvasiddhipradāya** ...giver of fulfillment*
***Sarvatanayāya** ...the son of Śiva*
***Śarvarīpriyāya** ...loved by Pārvatī*
***Sarvātmakāya** ...the soul of all*
***Sṛishṭikartre** ...the creator*
***Devāya** ...the resplendent one*
***Anekārchitāya** ...worshiped by multitudes*
***Śivāya** ...the auspicious one*
***Śuddhāya** ...the pure one*
***Buddhipriyāya** ...who loves intelligence*
***Śāntāya** ...the peaceful one*
***Brahmachāriṇe** ...the celibate one*
***Gajānanāya** ...the elephant's faced*
***Dvaimāturāya** ...who has two mothers*
***Munistutāya** ...who is praised by sages*
***Bhaktavighna vināśanāya** ...who destroys devotees' obstacles*
***Ekadantāya** ...who has one tusk*
***Chaturbāhave** ...who has four arms*
***Chaturāya** ...the ingenious one*
***Śaktisaṁyutāya** ...united with power*
***Lambodarāya** ...who has a large belly*
***Śūrpakarṇāya** ...with fan-like ears*
***Haraye** ...destroys evil with lion-like courage*
***Brahmaviduttamāya** ...foremost knower of God*
***Kālāya** ...the master of destiny*
***Grahapataye** ...lord of planets*
***Kāmine** ...who is love*
***Somasūryāgni lochanāya** ...whose eyes are the moon, sun and fire*
***Pāśāṅkuśa dharāya** ...who holds a noose and a goad*
***Chaṇḍāya** ...who is fierce-looking*
***Guṇātītāya** ...who transcends qualities*
***Nirañjanāya** ...who is without blemish*
***Akalmashāya** ...who is without impurity*
***Svayaṁsiddhāya** ...self-fulfilled, perfect*

Siddhārchita padāmbujāya *...whose lotus feet sages worship*
Bījapūraphalāsaktāya *...who is fond of pomegranates*
Varadāya *...the boon giver*
Śāśvatāya *...the eternal, unchanging one*
Kṛitine *...the skillful one*
Dvijapriyāya *...fond of the twice-born*
Vītabhayāya *...who is fearless*
Gadine *...who wields the mace*
Chakriṇe *...who wields a discus*
Ikshuchāpadhṛite *...who holds a sugarcane bow*
Śrīdāya *...the bestower of wealth*
Ajāya *...the unborn one*
Utpalakarāya *...who holds a proud blue lotus flower*
Śrīpataye *...the Lord of wealth*
Stutiharshitāya *...who delights in praise*
Kulādribhṛite *...who supports Himālaya, His family's mountain*
Jaṭilāya *...who has matted hair*
Kalikalmasha nāśanāya *...the destroyer of sins in the Kaliyuga*
Chandrachūḍāmaṇaye *...who wears a moon upon his head*
Kāntāya *...the beloved, loving one*
Pāpahāriṇe *...the consumer of sins*
Samāhitāya *...absorbed in meditation*
Āśritāya *...who is our refuge*
Śrīkarāya *...who manifests prosperity*
Saumyāya *...the amiable one*
Bhaktavāñçhita dāyakāya *...the grantor of devotees' desires*
Śāntāya *...the peaceful one*
Kaivalya sukhadāya *...bestower of unsullied liberation*
Sacchidānanda vigrahāya *...embodiment of existence-knowledge-bliss*
Jñānine *...the great wisdom*
Dayāyutāya *...full of compassion*
Dāntāya *...who has self-control*
Brahmadvesha vivarjitāya *...who is free from aversion to knowledge*

Pramattadaitya bhayadāya *...who brings terror to demons*
Śrīkaṇṭhāya *...with beautiful throat*
Vibudheśvarāya *...Lord of the Wise*
Rāmārchitāya *...worshiped by Rāma*
Vidhaye *...who is the destiny of all*
Nāgarāja yajñopavītavate *...whose sacred thread is a king cobra*
Sthūlakaṇṭhāya *...of stout neck*
Svayaṁkartre *...who is self-created*
Sāmaghoshapriyāya *...who loves the sound of Sāma Veda*
Parasmai *...who is supreme*
Sthūlatuṇḍāya *...who has a stout trunk*
Agraṇye *...the leader*
Dhīrāya *...the courageous one*
Vāgīśāya *...the Lord of speech*
Siddhidāyakāya *...bestower of fulfillment*
Dūrvābilva priyāya *...who loves dūrvā grass and bilva leaves*
Avyaktamūrtaye *...the manifestation of the Unmanifest*
Adbhutamūrtimate *...of wondrous form*
Śailendratanujotsaṅga khelanotsukamānasāya *...who is happy to play in the lap of His mother, Pārvatī, daughter of the mountain Lord*
Svalāvaṇyasudhāsārajita manmathavigrahāya *...who defeated Manmatha, the God of love, by His sweet beauty*
Samasta jagadādhārāya *...the supporter of all the worlds*
Māyine *...the source of illusory power*
Mūshikavāhanāya *...who rides the mouse*
Hṛishṭāya *...the joyful one*
Tushṭāya *...the contented one*
Prasannātmane *...the bright kindly-souled one*
Sarvasiddhi pradāyakāya *...the grantor of all fulfillment*

XIV. Mantra Pushpam Worship with Flowers

Aum yo-pām pushpam veda,
pushpavān prajāvān paśumān bhavati,
chandramāvā apām puspam
puspavān prajāvān paśumān bhavati,
ya evaṁ veda, yo-pāmāyatanaṁ veda,
āyatanavān bhavati.

Aum Śrī Mahāgaṇeśvarāya namaḥ mantra pushpāñjaliṁ samarpayāmi

The one who understands the beauty of the blooming powers of the Supreme Being is blessed with beautiful, blooming life, progeny and cattle. The moon is certainly the bloom of those powers. One who realizes the qualities of the moon, which are nothing but the blooming divine powers, is blessed with a blooming, beautiful life of perfection, progeny and cattle. One who realizes this principle and realizes the source from whom all these powers have come himself becomes the abode of those divine powers. Aum, salutations, Lord Mahāgaṇeśa, we respectfully offer you this flower mantra.

While chanting this mantra, hold a handful of flowers before you in añjali mudrā, hands cupped loosely around the flowers at chest height. Recite the verses with adoration. As you intone the last word, samarpayāmi, lower your hands and toss the flowers into the air above the murti, sending a shower of blossoms upon the God with feelings of gratitude and loving devotion.

XV. *Āratī Worship with Flame*

aum sājyaṁ trivartisaṁyuktam vahninā yojitaṁ mayā,
gṛihāṇa maṅgalāratim īśa putra namo-stu te.

aum āvāhitābhyaḥ sarvābhyo devatābhyo namaḥ
divya maṅgaladīpaṁ sandarśayāmi
āchamanīyaṁ samarpayāmi
maṅgalākshatān samarpayāmi

O Gaṇapati, Son of God Śiva, please accept this auspicious *āratī* prepared by me with ghee, three wicks and fire. My salutations to you! Aum! Salutations to all the Gods invoked! This divine, auspicious light we offer to you. After that, we offer you pure water for sipping and auspicious unbroken rice.

During this chant, hold the lit oil lamp or camphor burner in your right hand and the bell in your left. While ringing the bell and slowly reciting the āratī mantra, make three circles clockwise before Gaṇeśa with the flame. Stop at the top of the third circle, lower the lamp slightly and trace the symbol of Aum in Sanskṛit or in your native language. Then lift the flame slightly above the Aum that you placed in the ākāśic ether and ring the bell louder for all three worlds to hear. Keep ringing loudly while chanting the above two-line salutation to the devas ("āvāhitābhyaḥ ... sandarśayāmi"). Put down the bell and the lamp and then, with the flame still burning, offer a spoonful of water with "āchamanīyaṁ samarpayāmi," then a pinch of rice with "maṅgalāshatān samarpayāmi."

XVI. Rakshadhāraṇam Prayer for Protection

indra-stomena pañchadaśena
madhyamidaṁ vātena sagareṇa
raksha rakshām dhārayāmi

O Indra, Lord of material and spiritual prosperity, please protect the space between the heavens and earth as well as the mind between the body and the soul with the help of fifteen noble powers and virtues (five *prāṇas,* five *jñānendriyas* and five *karmendriyas).* Your protection and blessings sustain me.

As you recite this mantra, make three circles above the burning flame with a flower held in the right hand, stem upward. With the last words, toss the flower gently toward the Deity and place your hands in añjali mudrā while facing the altar. Now offer the flame at chest level to all present, allowing each to draw both hands through it and lightly touch the eyes three times. The Gods and devas can see us through the flame and send blessings. If especially honored persons are present, such as one's guru, parents or teacher, take the flame first to them. Then proceed clockwise to the others. In some cases, the pujārī may stand near the altar while devotees come forward to receive the flame. If no one is attending the pūjā, you may personally draw blessings from the flame, but not otherwise. Finally, present the flame once more to the Deity, then extinguish it with a wave of the right hand or by snuffing it out with a flower.

XVII. Arpaṇam Final Consecration

anayā yathā śakti kṛita
(state period of day from Saṅkalpam, above)
pūjayā bhagavān sarva devātmakaḥ
śrī mahāgaṇeśvaraḥ suprītaḥ
suprasanno varado bhavatu

To the best of our ability we have performed this (state time of day) pūjā and worshiped you, dear Lord, the brightest of all the Gods. May it please you. May it be enjoyed by you. Surrounded by your presence, we place ourselves in your care, loving Gaṇeśa.

Before reciting the above verse, place a pinch of rice in your left palm, then transfer it to the right palm. Add to the rice three spoonfuls of water and close the hand. Hold the rice before you as you face the Deity, the left hand under the right hand, and recite the mantra. As you intone the last words, let the rice and water fall into the tīrtha cup. The sacraments may then be given out in the following order: holy ash, blessed water, sandalpaste, red powder, food and flowers. If no one is attending the pūjā, you may partake of the sacraments yourself, but not otherwise. If many devotees are attending, a second person may help pass out the sacraments, except for the holy ash, which is always given by the person who performed the pūjā.

XVIII. Visarjanam Farewell and Apologies

Aum āvāhanaṁ na jānāmi na jānāmi visarjanam,
pūjāñchaiva na jānāmi kshamyatām parameśvara.
mantrahīnaṁ kriyāhīnam bhaktihīnaṁ sureśvara,
yat pūjitam mayā deva paripūrṇam tadastu te,
anyathā śaraṇaṁ nāsti tvameva śaraṇam mama,
tasmāt kāruṇyabhāvena raksha raksha gaṇeśvara.
Aum tat sat Aum.

O Lord, we do not know the proper means of inviting you or, when taking our leave, how to wish you farewell. A full knowledge of priestly rites has not been imparted to us, so you must overlook and forgive any mistakes or omissions. We know little of mantras or pious conduct, and we are strangers to true bhakti. Nonetheless, please forgive us and regard our attempts as exact and complete—because you are our only refuge. With your compassionate nature, Lord Gaṇeśa, we beseech you, please protect those who pray. That which is Truth is Aum.

This concluding apology is recited with hands in añjali mudrā. It is a formal and devout end to the worship service. As the final words, "Aum tat sat Aum," are spoken, it is customary to clap your hands together three times. All may now prostrate.

It is traditional and most uplifting to meditate for a few minutes after the pūjā, rather than rushing offer to daily duties. There is great personal benefit in such internalized worship, eyes closed, mind still, following, deep within yourself, the prāṇas that the pūjā has created. Externalized worship is the bhakti path; internalized worship is the yoga path. Both together make the complete circle that sustains devotees in their spiritual life, making them strong and kindly in moving the forces of the world in their daily life. This dual-pronged effort towards self-transformation and right living is the very foundation for the final goal of all seekers: moksha, freedom from rebirth.

Endnotes

1. J.C. Chatterji discusses the relationship between the three gunas and liberation in *The Wisdom of the Vedas*. (Wheaton, Ill.: Quest Books, 1992 (61-62). Chaterjee says that *rajas* literally means "flaring up like red fire or dust" while *sattva* means "existence" and *tamas* means "darkness." The *rajasic* person expends energy to secure worldly ends, while the *tamasic* person harms self or others for gain. Ultimately, the yogi seeks to go beyond all three gunas, but the quality of *sattva* can be an aid along the way.
2. See Kazanas, N.D. "Indo-European Deities and the Îgveda." Journal of Indo-European Studies 20, 3 &4 (Fall and Winter, 2001).
3. See Coomaraswamy, Ananda. "Ganesha." *Bulletin of the Museum of Fine Arts,* Boston. Vol. 26, No. 154 (1928): p. 30.
4. Subramaniyaswami, Satguru Satyananda. Loving Ganesha: Hinduism's Endearing Elephant-Faced God. Kapaa, HI: Himalayan Academy, 2000. See Ch. 6.
5. Forum for Hindu Awakening. www.forumforhinduawakening.org
6. Rumi often used the imagery of drunkenness in his devotional poetry. See *The Essential Rumi.* Translation by Coleman Barks with John Moyne. New York: Harper, 1997. St. Augustine's encounter with a drunken Milan beggar played a part in his conversion (*Confessions,* Translated by Henry Chadwick VI, p. 97, Oxford: Oxford University Press, 1991).
7. The "now" recalls the younger Ram Dass in *Remember Be Here Now* (Hanuman Foundation, 1971) and the older, more touching Ram Dass portrayed in the documentary "Ram Dass: Fierce Grace" (Independent Lens, 2001). The now, as I use it, perhaps owes more to Martin Buber's *I and Thou*

(Translated by Walter Kaufmann, New York: Simon and Schuster, 1970).

8. Diogenes and Montaigne held versions of this belief. See Gilbert Murray. *Five Stages of Greek Religion*. 3rd edition. Mineola, NY: Dover, 2002. Montaigne, Michel de. *The Essays: A Selection*. Translated by M.A. Screech. New York, Penguin, 2004.
9. Sri Dharma Pravartaka Acharya (Dr. Frank Morales), paraphrasing the Vedas, often says that "Dharma protects those who serve dharma." www.dharmacentral.com.
10. *Tao Te Ching*. Translated by Victor H. Mair. New York: Bantam, 1998. 46 (2), p. 60.
11. See Mark 8: 18
12. (*Shivastotravali*, song 1, v. 10, v. 15, pp. 30-31) Bailly, Constantina Rhodes. *Shaiva Devotional Songs of Kashmir: A Translation and Study of Utpaladeva's Shivastotravali.* Albany: State University of New York Press, 1987.

MANTRA
BOOKS

We publish books on Eastern religions and philosophies. Books that aim to inform and explore the various traditions, that began rooted in East and have migrated West.

9781780990996